MAGIC

MAGIC

Earvin "Magic" Johnson
and Richard Levin

The Viking Press   *New York*

*To my mother and father and to the memories
of my grandmother and Reggie Chastine*
Earvin "Magic" Johnson

To Baby James and the magic in him
Richard Levin

Copyright © 1983 by Earvin Johnson and Richard Levin
All rights reserved

First published in 1983 by The Viking Press
40 West 23rd Street, New York, N.Y. 10010

Published simultaneously in Canada by
Penguin Books Canada Limited

Library of Congress Cataloging in Publication Data
Johnson, Earvin, 1959–
Magic.
1. Johnson, Earvin, 1959–
2. Basketball players—United States—Biography.
I. Levin, Richard. II. Title.
GV884.J63A35 1983   796.32'3'0924 [B]   82-42741
ISBN 0-670-44804-4

Set in Video Gael
Printed in the United States of America

Contents

Author's Note
What follows is my best recollection of the people, events, places and experiences recounted. Some of the statements that appear as quotations have been paraphrased; however, all of the statements accurately reflect the substance of what was said.

MAGIC

1

The Challenge
TRAINING CAMP—1981–82

October 30, 1981

This morning was warm and windy. I wiped the sweat from my forehead as I stepped out the front door of my apartment and headed downstairs to the garage. The wind in the air reminded me more of Lansing, Michigan, my hometown, than Los Angeles. But I didn't mind the weather. It could have been snowing, for all I cared. I was just glad it was October 30.

Basketball season, at last. My season.

There's a lot I want to prove this year. I still have flashes, like nightmares, about the game that knocked us out of the playoffs last season. I missed the shot that could have won it for us and for the first time in my life people were saying I choked. If there's anything I really hate in life, it's losing. I didn't sleep much that night. I kept playing the game over and over again in my mind and it always came out the same: Lakers losers by a point. A lot of people around the league were happy to see us lose. This year those smiles are going to fade, because the Los Angeles Lakers are going to be champions again.

Overall, last season was a disaster for me. First, surgery for torn knee cartilage kept me out of action three and a half months. I had never been seriously injured before and it shocked me. I was playing well and with great confidence. I was on a high, still flying from the previous season, my rookie year, when we had won the Pacific Division title and then went on to take Philadelphia in six games for the league championship.

Then—boom—I wreck my knee while trying to make a defensive cut in a game against Kansas City in mid-November. It was like somebody had grabbed me by the scruff of the neck and said, "Easy, Earvin. Not so fast."

By the time I rejoined the Lakers late in the season, everything was different. And it had nothing to do with my knee. That felt okay, although I was being less than truthful by telling everybody it was 95 percent healed.

The team wasn't the same. It had gone through changes during my absence, some of which were difficult. The closeness of the championship season was gone, replaced by tension. Everybody seemed more distant, more withdrawn. No overt hostility, but I could sense an uneasiness. When you play team sports all your life, as I have, you develop a sense of team. You immediately know if something or somebody is out of line. You can feel it, and on the night of February 27, 1981, when I returned, I felt it.

It's the job of a team's publicity and promotions departments to generate as much interest in the team as possible. Interest means ticket sales. So when a date was set for my comeback, the people who run these departments for the Lakers began hyping the news: "Magic is coming back." On the night of the game—against the New Jersey Nets—they gave away "Magic" sweat suits and "The Magic Is Back" souvenir buttons. They drew 17,505—the Lakers' first sell-out since my injury.

Sportswriters came in from all over the country. At shoot-around that morning, broadcasters descended on me.

"Magic, how's the knee?"

"Fine."

"Magic, do you think the Lakers can win another title?"

"I hope so."

"Magic, how's it feel to be back?"

"Great."

"Magic, how do you feel about not starting right away?"

"That's how it should be."

"Magic, what kind of adjustments will the Lakers have to make?"

"Some, but not too many. They know me. It's not like I'm a new player."

"Magic, look into the camera."

I looked into the camera.

"Magic, smile."

I smiled.

After shoot-around, cameramen followed me home. They wanted to record every moment on film. Why? I'll never know. I had to turn them down. I told them I had to go to bed and rest, which I did. But when I left my apartment to go to the Forum that evening, the cameramen were waiting. More met me at the Forum. They followed me into the locker room and kept the cameras rolling as I dressed for the game.

My teammates didn't express any displeasure, but they were obviously distracted. The members of the media interviewed Kareem Abdul-Jabbar, Norm Nixon, Jamaal Wilkes, and Paul Westhead, the head coach. I didn't hear the questions or answers, but I'm sure the questions concerned my return and the effect it would have on the team, and I am equally sure the answers were polite and positive.

Finally, the trainer, Jack Curran, on word from Westhead

threw everybody out, leaving us alone for the first time. The locker room became quiet. The players already had welcomed me back, which was nice, but instinctively I'd felt their gestures carried more courtesy than warmth.

If they were upset, I understood. All the newspapers were saying that now that I was healthy I was going to lead them to another championship. Certainly the guys felt my return helped their chances. But I don't think they appreciated the illusion—"The Magic Is Back"—that I was going to do it by myself.

They also resented the lack of credit and recognition for their considerable achievements in my absence. Immediately after my injury, they'd had to make two important adjustments. First, guard Norm Nixon began quarterbacking the team on a full-time basis. It was a job he'd handled before I became a Laker and one we'd shared since I became one. Second, Kareem, one of the greatest basketball players who ever lived, had to reassert himself after beginning the season slowly. These adjustments took time. They lost 5 of their first 8 games and 11 of their first 22. They began playing well by the first of the year and won 17 of the next 23 games, giving them a 28–17 record without me. They were proud of what they did, and rightly so, even if nobody seemed to notice. Worse, nobody seemed to care. Attendance at the Forum declined.

On the night I returned, once the locker room was cleared out Westhead delivered his normal pregame talk. As some players stretched and limbered up, he discussed individual match-ups, went over a few of the New Jersey plays, explained what we should try to do, and stressed that winning this game was important if we hoped to catch Phoenix and win the Pacific Division championship.

Westhead didn't say anything to me. He had talked to me earlier in the day.

"I'll put you in towards the end of the first period," he had said. "Then we'll see how it goes from there."

I'd nodded. "That's fine, Coach."

"I don't think we should bring you along too quickly."

"Whatever you think is best."

Although Westhead is an extremely intelligent and well-read man who lectured in college and has gained a reputation for being a Shakespearean scholar, he doesn't communicate well with the players. He tells you what to do and that's it. He doesn't tell you why or even present the big picture, which might put plans in better perspective. In that respect, he is from the old school and is more like a college coach than an NBA coach. He keeps his emotions in check and never rips or praises a player after a game. Occasionally he'll pull a player to one side and say a few words.

I knew it was going to be a big night, but I was still stunned by the noise of the crowd as we ran out for our pregame warm-ups. There were 17,505 people out there. A sellout against the New Jersey Nets. It was like a season opener, or a championship final. I felt good. I was back.

Then came the introductions of players. They announced me first.

"From Michigan State . . . a six-nine guard . . . Magic Johnson."

The crowd went crazy. I smiled and nodded and stood on the free-throw line and waited for the cheering to die down. I waited, and I waited some more. It wouldn't stop. I looked at the bench and saw the guys shaking their heads in amazement. I felt naked out there. Just me and a dozen or so photographers. One of them tried to say something to me, but I couldn't hear over the noise. Not knowing what else to do, I finally spread my arms out in front of me as if to say, "What did I do to deserve this?"

The game itself was anticlimactic as well as poorly played. It was obvious we were distracted. And it was just as obvious that a few significant adjustments would be required. At one point Norm and I almost collided in the backcourt. I assumed we would share the point-guard position as we did before, but now he was so used to handling it that he instinctively tried to beat me to the ball to run a play.

"That's okay, Norman," I told him as we stopped and talked for a couple of seconds. It must have looked funny to the fans.

"No, I'll take it," he said.

"Okay." I gave it up and set up at the off-guard position.

We struggled all night, but still managed to win. I was nervous when I entered the game in the first period and turned the ball over a few times. As the game wore on, I relaxed and grew more confident. Towards the end, I made two important plays, one a rebound and the other an assist to Nixon. When it was over, I felt relieved. I had passed an important test. I could play.

The locker room was crazy—wall-to-wall people. Reporters asked me the same questions they'd asked before the game. The answers didn't change much. Since most of the attention was focused on me, the others dressed and got out of there as quickly as possible. Some didn't make it fast enough and were questioned by reporters.

Norm's comments were typical.

"Incredible," he said. "I've never seen so many cameras in one place in all my life. This was bigger than winning the championship. I'll never forget the standing ovation Magic got before the game."

He made it a point to say that neither he nor any of the others resented the publicity I got.

"Not at all," he said. "If anything, we're happy to see somebody get it who deserves it."

If Nixon's comments were typical of what the others were saying, Jim Chones's may have been typical of what they were feeling.

"I thought it was bullshit," he said. "It was a circus."

Chones surprised me. He was a veteran who certainly understood the business aspects of the game. He knew what hype was all about, having experienced it himself as a major star at Marquette in the early seventies and later in the old American Basketball Association, where he was one of the league's highest-paid players and hyped as the next Kareem. Besides, Jim was my friend.

There were seventeen games remaining in the 1980–81 season. Enough time to make the necessary adjustments and be sharp for the playoffs. Enough time to put away our egos and petty irritations and become a team again. But it didn't happen right away.

I wasn't in tune. I wasn't included in the conversations anymore. For the first time in my life, I felt like the odd man out, which was hard for me to accept. I'm a gregarious person. I love to talk and jive with the guys. While I'd missed playing basketball, I think I missed being around the guys even more. Now I was back and I still didn't feel like one of the guys. It was hard for me to accept. And what was even more puzzling was that I didn't believe it was intentional. It was partly that because I'd missed so much of the season, I simply could not share the frustrations and anxieties the others had experienced. I was like a free agent picked up at the end of the year, a newcomer who can't relate because he didn't fight the same battles.

Through the first week, I tried to feel my way. It was like walking on eggshells. I was sensitive to everybody's feelings, and the last thing I wanted to happen was to say something and have somebody come back with "Hey, who is this guy? He returns after all this time and expects everything to be the same. Wrong." It was strange, like it was eleven against one, them against me. By the end of the month we'd loosened up and were playing well. Then— right before the start of the playoffs—all hell broke loose.

It started with a newspaper story in which Norman was quoted as saying that I was taking away his game. The story appeared just before our playoff opener—the best-of-three mini-series against the Houston Rockets, a team with a losing record whom we rightly were expected to beat.

I didn't read the story. In fact, I didn't even know about it until the next day, when reporters and friends began asking me about it. I was really burned. I mean, I've never taken anybody's game away. I'd thought Norman and I had worked out our individual responsibilities during my rookie season: whoever has the ball takes it, and the other guy goes. It's simple and it works. But if he wanted the ball, he could have it. I didn't care. I was mad, really mad. Here I was coming off a serious injury, playing as hard as I could and trying to help the team win, and this was what I got. I just want to win. That's all I care about. If I have to rebound, I'll go out and get 15; if the team needs assists, I'll pass; if it needs scoring, I'll go for 30. I don't care about points and who's handling the ball. If somebody's man gets by him, I'm going to switch and help out, just as I hope somebody will be there to save me in a similar situation. That's what basketball is all about; it's a team game in which players work together and, hopefully, create a situation where the whole is greater than the sum of the parts. But that can't happen when a player goes public and points a finger at a teammate.

The article was a smack in the face. Norman not only implied that I hog the ball, but that I hog publicity and endorsements as well. So when reporters asked me for a response, I was candid. I told them this was the first time I'd ever experienced team dissension and I didn't like it.

"We've become a bunch of individuals," I said. "We didn't have ego problems last year. We put that stuff behind us. But now everybody spends more time worrying about getting his share and what the other guy is getting than with winning games.

"There are some guys who resent the publicity and endorsements I get. They think I hog it all. But the companies come to me, I don't go to them. The same thing with publicity. I don't write those stories."

Well, that did it.

Houston who?

We didn't battle the Rockets; we battled ourselves. Our

heads were never into the mini-series. All we talked about—in the locker room, in airports, on buses—were the newspaper stories. Everything was happening too quickly. Norm and I were good friends and eventually talked about the conflict at length, but, unfortunately, we didn't resolve it until after we had lost to Houston. The repercussions, as might be expected, were widespread. Everybody went into a shell and carefully watched what he said for fear of being overheard, quoted, misquoted, misinterpreted, or whatever. The other players didn't know if Norm had been quoted accurately or not, even though he denied it. They didn't know what was going through my head, either, and they resented the fact that I said they resented me. What a mess. In retrospect, besides being dumb, it was contrived, but it was very real at the time. Everybody was waiting to see what was going to be in the papers next.

Incredible as it may seem, we were even hashing it out in the locker room before going on the floor for the final game with the mini-series tied 1–1. Some of the players interpreted my response to Norm's story as a signal that my ego was tripping out, which was never my intent. I felt bad about that and told them so. None of us handled it very well.

All of this had more to do with our elimination from the playoffs than the Rockets did. I know my head wasn't into the final game. I made only two of fourteen shots. I missed two of three free throws with thirty seconds to go. And I shot an air ball, of all things, in the final seconds, while putting up the shot that could have won the game. It was the worst game of my life.

Although I was down in the dumps and greatly disappointed afterwards, I was relieved that the incredible pressure was gone. I went home, then went out to dinner and spent the night playing whist with a couple of friends.

I took a lot of criticism over the next few days for taking the last shot instead of passing to Kareem the way Coach Westhead had diagrammed the play. Everybody knew Westhead had called Kareem's number because CBS had a camera and boom mike in the huddle. Well, I would have gotten the ball to Kareem under ideal conditions. But ideal conditions seldom exist during a game. When you are on a basketball floor, or any athletic field, you must react instinctively and with good judgment.

Just as fans all over the country knew we wanted to go in to Kareem for the final shot, so did the Rockets, and they didn't need a television set. When play resumed after the time-out, I took a look at the defense to see what it was going to give us. And it wasn't going to give us Kareem. He was being double-teamed. I came down the middle, dribbling with my left hand while watching Kareem, waiting for him to make his move. We were both indecisive. He was watching and waiting for me, too. Finally, when I went, he went. After seeing the videotape, I decided that I might have been able to get him the pass, but I didn't think so at the time. I thought I had a good shot and that was it. You go for what you know. I drove the middle and was right where I wanted to be. As I went up, Tom Henderson of the Rockets went with me. Normally I lean in on the shot, but this time, thinking Henderson might have position to take a charge, I leaned back. I don't know why I did, because I never do. I came up short and Moses Malone grabbed the rebound. That was the game and the season.

Most accounts of the game weren't very kind to me. Some reporters suggested the magic was gone. One called me Tragic Johnson. It goes with the territory.

Dr. Jerry Buss, the owner of the Lakers, telephoned me the next day. He wanted to talk. He invited me to join him at the Ocotillo Lodge, a hotel he owns in Palm Springs.

Dr. Buss, who earned a doctorate in chemistry at the University of Southern California, made his money in the Southern California real estate market, beginning in 1959. He and his partner, Frank Mariani, parlayed an investment of $1,000 each into hundreds of millions. He is smart, ambitious, and extremely competitive. He makes no bones about it. He does not like to lose and is not very good at it. He likes to say, "Good losers are by definition losers."

This loss was no exception. He said he wanted to talk to me because I was one of the few who could comprehend the depth of emotion he was experiencing.

He arranged a picnic in a beautiful wooded area in Idyll-wild, about twenty miles southwest of Palm Springs.

"What happened between you and Norm?" he asked.

"I don't really know," I said. "Norm and I haven't had a chance to sit down and talk it out. You read the story, didn't you?"

He nodded.

"Norm said it was taken out of context," I said. I shrugged. "So I really don't know."

"Do you take away from his game?"

"To some extent, yes. Just as to some extent he takes away from my game. That's the way it is. It's pretty natural. I guess that's what he means when he says he was quoted out of context."

"Can you and Norm play together?"

I nodded. "Definitely."

Buss was quiet for a few moments. I looked around. It was pretty in the meadow. The birds were chirping, the grass was lush, the skies cloudless, the air clean and clear. It was nice being in the country, away from the noise, the hustle of Los Angeles.

"If you could play with any guard in the NBA," he continued, "regardless of the cost and how he might be obtained, who would he be?"

"Norm Nixon," I said.

"Why?"

"Because he's the quickest. I need his quickness; it makes me much more effective. I'm too big. Norm, with that incredible quickness, adds a dimension to my game that nobody else can."

"That's interesting," he said.

We then went on and discussed Laker weaknesses and what might be done to improve the team. He asked me if I thought Mitch Kupchak would help.

"Get him," I said.

Kupchak, a true power forward at six foot ten, 230 pounds, played his first five years as a pro with the Washington Bullets, mostly in the shadow of Elvin Hayes and Wes Unseld. Still, he was a respected player and was on the verge of becoming a free agent.

We needed a power forward, and Kupchak was considered the best power forward among the free agents. Buss was intent on signing him, regardless of the cost, which he expected to be astronomical. But first he wanted to clean up the mess left from our loss to Houston. So he set up a meeting with me and Norm.

We met at the Sands Hotel in Las Vegas several weeks later. I arrived from Lansing; Norm and Dr. Buss flew in on separate flights from Los Angeles. Dr. Buss arranged a lavish brunch in his suite the following morning: eggs, ham, sausage, bacon, potatoes, fruit, lox, bagels, whitefish, cream cheese, juice, the works.

As Norm and I began piling food on our plates, Buss got down to business.

"Look," he said, "I don't understand, so you guys have to tell me."

He looked directly at Norman.

"Do you play well together? Does Magic attract too much attention from you, Norman? What does it mean that he needs the ball to perform and you need the ball to perform? What do you guys want to do? Let's be honest about it. Because if he's hurting you, Norman, honestly I can trade you to any team in the league. Absolutely and positively you can choose wherever it is you want to play, because you are so good there isn't a team in the league that doesn't want you. So, if you're having problems, tell me."

Norm was finishing a wedge of melon. He shook his head.

"Wrong," he said. "There is no problem. There is no

jealousy. Whoever should have the ball is the guy who can help us win. If that's me, that's great. If that's Magic, that's great, too. If it's both of us, then great. I love Los Angeles, and I love playing for the Lakers. I want to stay.

"I don't know how the story came out. You know how it is. They ask you questions and keep asking you the same questions. Somewhere along the line something gets into the papers that does not reflect the true meaning in which it was originally said. But what can you do about it? Deny it? If you say 'I didn't mean for it to come out like that,' then it sounds like you're constantly backing down from things.

"Magic and I have never had any problems in the past, and I don't see why we should have any in the future. What happened was the exception, not the rule."

"Hey, Norm," I said, "would you stop eating all my fruit?" Everybody laughed.

What had to be said was said. We talked for another three or four hours and still couldn't finish all the food. The discussion was mostly lighthearted. We even joked about how ridiculous and paranoid everybody had acted during the playoffs, ourselves included. I returned to Lansing later that day looking forward to a nice, laid-back summer. I was happy the conflict with Norm had been resolved.

But the peace didn't last long. I had become a Laker for life by signing an extension to my contract a few weeks after the season ended. The terms, the exact dollar amounts in particular, were not supposed to be revealed. After the extension was signed, it was sent to the league office in New York for approval, as all player agreements are. The Lakers then planned to make a formal announcement at a press conference at the Forum.

It would have gone something like this: "The Lakers have signed Magic Johnson to an extension of his present contract which expires following the 1983–84 season. It is a multiyear, multimillion-dollar agreement covering the length of his professional basketball career."

The media would have had a field day speculating about how much and for how long. There would have been some great rumors. But eventually a reasonable figure would have been agreed to and the media would have gone on to something else. From then on, you would have read: "Magic Johnson, who makes an estimated blah-blah . . ." Since the NBA does not release player salaries, most of the figures you hear and read about are wrong.

Unfortunately, the press conference never came to pass. Shortly after the contract was sent to the league, rumors began making the rounds. I was taking summer classes at Michigan State University and playing softball, so I didn't pay any attention to them. The Lakers did, however. They were upset because the rumors implied that the new agreement would take effect immediately, which meant it was a renegotiation and not an extension. Dr. Buss, like most other owners, had gone on record saying he would never renegotiate a contract. But even more upsetting to the Lakers was the impression that I would be making more money than Kareem Abdul-Jabbar, the team captain and superstar. One strictly enforced rule on the Lakers is that Kareem remains Number One. The terms of my contract did not violate that rule.

After successfully dodging rumors for a week, Dr. Buss found himself trapped by a cable-television interviewer. Surprised by the knowledge of the reporter, he simply answered yes to the questions put to him.

He answered yes to: "Did you sign Magic to an extension to his present contract that expires at the end of the 1983–84 season?"

Yes to: "Is it one million dollars a year for twenty-five years?"

Yes to: "Is it a personal-services contract guaranteed by you and not the Lakers?"

And yes to: "Will Magic continue to work for you, perhaps in a basketball-related capacity, after his playing days are over?"

The story exploded. I felt like I was in the middle of an earthquake. Dr. Buss was interviewed late in the afternoon, Los Angeles time, and my telephone was ringing off the hook in Lansing, Michigan, by mid-evening. My initial reaction was shock, because we had agreed never to release the figures.

Buss later told me he didn't realize he was the primary source of the story. He assumed the information was common knowledge because of leaks out of New York, which he knew about, and because of the accuracy of the reporter's information.

"I just kept saying 'Yes, that's true' to his questions," Dr. Buss said. "I thought the New York papers must have obtained a copy of the contract. I had no idea I was releasing information that up to that point had not been verified. It's difficult sometimes to keep a secret. While it clearly is in everyone's best interests to do certain things secretly, I, for one, have never been able to answer falsely when asked a direct question. I can't lie to protect a secret. I guess in order of priorities, secrecy to me is second to truthfulness."

How can you argue with that?

Nonetheless, Dr. Buss did not entirely clear up the matter. Three misconceptions continued to linger.

First, that I am currently being paid $1 million a year. I am being paid according to the terms of my original contract, a five-year deal signed in 1979.

Second, that I am obligated to Buss for twenty-five years. While the money is to be paid over that length of time, I am only obligated for a certain number of years, most of which, if not all, will be spent playing basketball for the Los Angeles Lakers.

And third, that I am part of management. Buss inadvertently raised this issue by suggesting that I might become coach or general manager of the Lakers, or even president of his overall sports company, after my playing career was over. I have no intention of doing any of those things—I don't even have any desire to do them.

While the contract itself neither mentions nor implies a future role in team management, either during or after my playing career, there were many—one being Kareem Abdul-Jabbar—who assumed it did. This hurt me, because I would never ask or expect to be treated any differently from my teammates.

At first I was totally unaware that Kareem was upset. He let it go for a month or so before arranging a meeting with Buss. I guess he couldn't take it any longer. The meeting was preceded by a nationwide media blitz. For a full week, there were rumors that Kareem wanted to be traded to New York.

I didn't know what was going on, but I had a feeling I was going to wind up right in the middle of the whole mess.

I opened my one-week summer basketball camp at Pepperdine University in Malibu the same day Kareem and his agents met Dr. Buss at the Forum. It was reported that Kareem told Buss he didn't understand what my contract meant. Was I management or was I labor? Kareem claimed he spoke on behalf of other members of the team but never identified them. When I learned about this, I was confused. I could not conceive how Kareem, a player who is smart and who understands the ins and outs of pro sports as well as anyone, could think even for a moment that I was part of management.

"No one that I know is suffering from any jealousy," Kareem said in a postmeeting press conference. "What concerns us is what his contract means as it was presented to us. As you know, a team is like a family. When you pick one person out and stand him in front of the others and say he's my favorite child, the rest of the family is affected. Nobody knew what was going on. Some of the players thought they had to compete for the affections of the owner besides doing their jobs on the basketball court. . . ."

I was equally surprised by Dr. Buss's reaction. He apologized publicly for the misunderstanding, claiming it was unintentional, and assured Kareem that my contract in no way set me apart from the others. I was a player, would continue to be one, and would continue to be subject to the same rules and regulations governing the others. He even commended Kareem for having the foresight to spot a potentially explosive situation and defuse it before anything happened.

My initial reaction was, "Oh, man, here we go again. First the thing with Norm, now this." Dr. Charles Tucker, my adviser, friend, and surrogate big brother all rolled into one, was helping me with the basketball camp when this came out.

"Tuck," I told him, "I'm getting tired of all this. I think maybe we should do something, maybe go play someplace else."

This was the morning after Kareem's meeting. We were sitting in a small, plain office in the Pepperdine athletic building. Down the hall, about three hundred kids were going through various drills on the basketball courts under the guidance of our staff of coaches. We were reading the newspaper accounts of the meeting. We knew a few reporters were already waiting in the gym and more were on the way.

Tuck shook his head. He didn't want to hear about any move. While he's a midwesterner at heart and will never leave his home in Lansing, he likes visiting Los Angeles several times a year.

"Nah," he said. "Let's just keep cool. I don't think people are taking it the right way."

I wasn't convinced of that, but I nodded anyway. I knew it wasn't wise to rush into anything without knowing all the facts.

"What do I tell the reporters?" I asked.

Tuck shrugged. "Tell them how you feel. Be honest about it."

I came out about noon. I went up to the balcony and leaned over the railing to watch the scene below. The kids were on the courts. My father and my attorneys, George and Harold Andrews, were there, too. Dozens of sportswriters, broadcasters, cameramen, technicians, and photographers wandered around the sidelines. You can always pick out the TV broadcasters. They are the ones wearing coats and ties and looking perfectly cool despite the weather. On this day it was hot, inside and out.

Once everybody was there, Bob Mazza, a Beverly Hills press agent who had arranged the press conference, guided the group into a nearby classroom. I took my place behind the lectern and waited for the inevitable question. This was one time I wasn't smiling.

"What's your reaction to yesterday's meeting between Kareem and Buss?"

"I'll tear it up if it's going to cause problems," I told them. I was talking about the contract and I was dead serious. I'm not in this for the money. I know people don't believe that. They think all athletes are greedy. Some are, to be sure, just as many people in other lines of work are greedy, but many aren't. Money is cool, and you have to have some to get by, but you don't see me with a big house in Bel Air or Beverly Hills; you don't see me wearing fancy clothes and showing diamonds and gold and rubies and stuff like that. I like cars, so I drive one that's comfortable and expensive, a Mercedes. Otherwise I don't spend much on myself. I help out my mom and dad, who still live in Lansing. I donate a lot to charities. The rest is invested on advice from my parents and my attorneys. I'm just not a big spender. All money means to me is that I can enjoy myself and not have to worry about it while playing ball.

Besides, I never went in and said, "Hey, I want twenty-five million dollars." Dr. Buss approached me. Neither he, nor I, wanted me to go through the circus of my someday becoming a free agent. And so we worked out the long-term deal.

Dr. Buss is a very shrewd man. Somehow there's an impression that luck has played an important role in his financial advancement—like he was lucky to start buying property in Santa Monica at the start of the real estate boom and—bam!—become a millionaire. But there were others who did the same thing he did, and they've faded away while he's endured and flourished. Moving money around is his business, and he's good at it. Take the financing of my contract. In order to guarantee it for twenty-five years, he capitalized on the interest rate, which was extremely high at the time he conceived the idea.

"The prime rate was a little over twenty percent, which I felt was an enormous sum of money," he explained once. "It dawned on me—and in my business you are continually thinking of ways to take advantage of abnormalities—I would reap one million dollars a year if I could put up five million dollars cash and lock up an annual interest rate of twenty percent."

He did not require the interest payments for another two years, so he set aside $3.5 million in a trust deed, arranged through a private party, and allowed the interest to accrue. By the time he began collecting the interest—and giving it to me—the principal would be slightly more than $5 million.

"One way to look at it is that I'm loaning you five million dollars, interest-free, which enables you to live off the interest for the next twenty-five years." Buss smiled when he told me that. He is sometimes amused by his own cleverness. He's willing to gamble. That's the heart of his success—in business and in high-stakes poker, his favorite pastime. One year after he made the trust-deed deal, the prime rate dropped significantly, so that if the same investment had been made later, it would have yielded $200,000 a year less. "A lot of it is timing," he says with pride. "I simply gambled. I said this is high and it's going to go lower. But it's a double-edged sword. If I lock myself in at twenty percent and it continues to rise, I get cut the other way."

• •

The first time I saw all my teammates together after signing the contract extension was October 1, Photo Day, the traditional beginning of training camp. In the parking lot outside the Los Angeles gym where we posed for photos, I drove by Kareem. He was getting out of his white Mercedes-Benz with blackout windows. I honked. He turned and waved.

I parked next to Jack Curran's van, which was loaded down with equipment. The rear doors were opened. Inside were a training table, boxes of tape, gauze, balm, Gatorade, chewing gum, wristbands, sweat socks, jocks, shorts, shirts, sneakers, shoelaces, knee braces, knee pads, knee sleeves, ankle wraps, home uniforms, road uniforms, cold tablets, and lots of aspirin. NBA trainers used to carry and administer prescription drugs, but the league became sensitive to drug abuse and stopped that several years ago. If a player needs prescribed medicine, he must get a prescription from a doctor.

I set my bag down next to the van and poked through the boxes.

"Get outta there."

It was Jack. His face was twisted up in a scowl and he was moving fast. The first day, and already he was running late.

Jack is a lovable, robust Irishman with reddish hair, reddish cheeks, and a reddish nose. When he's flushed, as he was then, he looks like a ball on fire. Although he takes great care of his players, which we appreciate, he can be a terror when his world isn't going as planned. He's threatened to pull "his" team off more airplanes and out of more hotels than I care to remember. While his tactics aren't especially delicate, somehow they get the job done.

"I was just looking for some gum," I told him.

"Why don't you ask?"

"Can I have some gum?"

Jack leaned into the back of the van, immediately pulled open the appropriate carton, and handed me a pack of spearmint.

"Here."

"You got a long season ahead of you."

"I know, and you guys are already busting my balls."

"Thanks for the gum, Jack."

"You're welcome."

Michael Cooper was parking his car. "Buck," he said as he came over.

Norm Nixon began calling me Buck—as in "young buck"—during my rookie season with the Lakers. Some of the guys picked up on it. They also call me Magic, Earvin, Earv, E, and E. J. I answer to them all.

Coop and I smacked hands and walked into the gym. We're tight. I spent a lot of time with Mike during my first training camp, in 1979. We got together for breakfast just about every morning and talked about how things were going, especially with him. His career was on the line, and he worried about it constantly. I kept pumping him up. "Coop," I'd tell him ten times every breakfast, "don't worry. You're going to make it. You're better than the guys you have to beat out." As it turned out, he was the last player to survive the final cut.

Now, two years later, Michael, a wiry, six foot six super leaper who plays two positions, off guard and small forward, doesn't worry about making the team. He is the best defensive guard and one of the best sixth men in the league. I call him Mr. Excitement for the way he turns on the fans with high-wire slam dunks, many off lob passes thrown by Norm or me. The press calls those plays "Coop-a-loops."

It was good to see all the guys again. Everybody was in a good mood as we put on our gold Laker uniforms with purple trim. We talked about our summers, and I let everybody know I'd had another sensational season at third base for the Magic Johnson Enterprises softball team. I hit nearly .600 against slow-pitch competition and informed the boys that I could do the same for the Dodgers.

"You'd have to take a pay cut," cracked Jim Brewer, one of our reserve power forwards.

"Yeah, Buck," piped up Jamaal Wilkes. "How about loaning me a couple hundred grand?"

I smiled. "Later," I told him.

The media, both print and electronic, attend Photo Day. Because of the nature of the event—a new season, a fresh start, things like that—the focus usually is on the future. Everybody talks about making the playoffs and possibly winning the championship. It is a time for hope and optimism.

This time, though, reporters kept bringing up the past: the last game against Houston, the conflict between Norm and me, and The Contract, which, I guess, should be capitalized because of the emotion it created.

I was short with my answers to questions about the contract during Photo Day. But I did go out of my way to tell the reporters that I bore no animosity towards Kareem for his intervention over the summer. There were no problems, I told them.

After Photo Day, I went home, packed my bags, and drove to Palm Springs for training camp. The team headquarters is the Ocotillo Lodge, the resort hotel owned by Dr. Buss. Each unit is a suite—a large bedroom, living room, bathroom, and kitchen with a small refrigerator and an apartment-size stove; outside is a private patio. Considering we're there ten days, it is an ideal setup. It provides us with plenty of room and privacy. There's a swimming pool and Jacuzzi, a recreation area, and a restaurant. We usually have the run of the place because early October is the off-season in Palm Springs and the whole city is dead.

I checked into my room, unpacked my bags, and headed up the street to the supermarket to load up on groceries. Although it was chilly and overcast 110 miles northwest, in Los Angeles, it was hot and dry here. In the market I ran into Jamaal Wilkes, whom we call Silk because of his smooth and graceful style. A couple of weeks earlier, he and his wife, Valerie, had suffered a horrible tragedy. Their daughter, Adrianne Julise, born less than a month before the opening of training camp, died suddenly. From crib death. She was eight days old.

Jamaal and I talked while waiting in line at the checkout counter. I had sent condolences earlier, but I hadn't had the opportunity to talk to him personally about it. I told him again how sorry I was.

"It's like a kick in the teeth," he said.

"How's Val doing?" I asked.

Silk shook his head. "Not too good. She's been kind of melancholy. She went home to visit her folks while we're here. That'll do her good."

"How about yourself?"

"I'm okay, I guess. Like I say, I feel like I've been kicked in the teeth."

"You got to be strong. I think the best thing to do is go right back and try again."

"You might be right," he said.

Training camp comes as a shock to the system. Hit a switch and suddenly you're on. Two-a-days right from the get-go. It shouldn't be called training camp. Nobody trains there. You come to camp already trained. If not, you are liable to get hurt. Years ago, players would use the time in camp to lose weight and get into shape. They'd start slowly and build up steam. No more. You start fast and go faster. Because of the great amounts of money involved and the intense competition for jobs, everybody arrives in peak physical condition. You can't afford not to.

Silk coasted through the first few days. His mind seemed to be wandering. Nobody said anything. We just let him be. He's a pro, and we knew he'd be ready when it was time. For the rest of us, it was bang time. We were hungry. We were embarrassed by the way we dropped out of the play-offs the year before. Everybody practiced hard, much harder than in previous camps, and with greater intensity. It didn't take long to realize we were going to be a better team. All it took was one look at Mitch Kupchak, our new power forward.

I felt sorry for the rookies—draft choices Mike McGee, Kevin McKenna, and Harvey Knuckles—and the free agents—Kurt Rambis and Clay Johnson. Kurt and Clay had been to pro camps before, but neither had survived the final cut. Kurt had tried out with the New York Knicks the year before and then wound up playing for a team in Athens, Greece. Clay was a draft choice of Portland in 1978. Ever since he's been a gypsy, playing for teams in the Continental League. They were shocked by the roughness. There is a world of difference between an NBA training camp and the various pro summer leagues, rookie camps, and minor leagues they had experienced. The guys here are bigger, tougher, smarter, more experienced, quicker, and just plain better. You don't get anything easy, especially after going head to head against the same players the first few days. At first the rookies and free agents stayed in the background, quiet and in awe. Then they got into it. It was as if they got together and decided, "They're banging us, so we better get down there and bang back." It turned out they were pretty good bangers, especially Kurt.

The fierce concentration and intense energy expended bring on complete exhaustion at the end of each day, so you tend to fall into the security of a set routine.

For example, I would get up at seven every morning, dress for practice—jock, shorts, jersey, sweat suit, and sneakers—and walk across the street to the coffee shop for breakfast. From there I'd go straight to Curran's room to get my ankles taped. I like to get there early. Jack has the rookies come in for a half hour beginning at eight, followed by the vets. I get there about 8:15. I like to jive with the younger guys; the conversations are different. Those guys, including the second-year players Butch Carter and Alan Hardy, get down and talk about serious business, like who's been waived, who's been traded, who's hurt, and who hasn't been waived. They wear out the scoreboard page of the sports section checking out the fine print under the heading TRANSACTIONS. It's like reading the obituaries.

The established vets come in sleepy-headed. They check out the transactions, too, but they also check out what's going on in the rest of the world of sports—like the Dodgers. A lot of us are Dodger fans. Eventually talk moves on to the workouts.

At this year's training camp, much of that talk was about the offensive system the coach, Paul Westhead, was implementing. Each day he introduced new play-sets. It got very confusing.

"Pass and pick, pass and pick," I was telling Norm while getting taped one day.

"I don't know what he's trying to do," Norm said. "Everybody's running into everybody else. Kupchak is so confused, he's out there tap dancing."

"I know it," I said. "I know it."

"Silk," said Norm. "You know what he's trying to do?"

Silk looked up from his newspaper and shook his head. "Nope," he said.

Every day, after I got taped, I returned to my room and listened to some R & B through my headphones. That's my way of concentrating. I'd leave for practice at 9:15. The drive from the Ocotillo Lodge to the College of the Desert in Palm Desert, where we practice, takes about ten minutes. It's all highway. The gym is a good one. Good floor, rims; it's roomy and air-conditioned, thank goodness. We'd be passing out right and left if we didn't have air-conditioning in the desert heat. Morning workouts were devoted mostly to drills and the new offense. They'd last from ten until noon. Then I'd head back to the Ocotillo. On the way, I'd stop at a fast food restaurant for a quick lunch, which I'd usually eat on the drive back. In the room, I'd ice down my knees and turn on the television and watch "Ironside" and then my man, Rockford. Sometimes I'd sit by the pool later in the afternoon, but mostly I'd stay inside and think about the morning workout. Eventually, I'd take a short nap.

The evening workout began at 5:30. Once again I'd get taped and drive to the College of the Desert. This workout would be more fun because we'd scrimmage the second hour. Some of the college crowd and people from the community would come out to watch, and we'd try our best to put on a show. Afterwards, we'd go back to the hotel and a team meeting.

The meeting would be held in a large room adjacent to the hotel lobby. Large platters of fruit would be set on each of the tables. Westhead used the time to review the day's workouts and to preview the next. After one week of camp we were still having problems with the new offense. Westhead stood by the blackboard and diagrammed the play-sets.

"You guys are not being patient enough," he said.

I raised my hand.

"Yes, E. J.," he said.

"I don't think that's it, Coach," I said. "I just don't think it's going to work."

"You guys are not running it," he snapped.

"We're all bumping into each other," I said.

Everybody was quiet. You could feel the tension in the room.

"Just run it, I don't want to hear any excuses," he said.

"It takes too long to get through all the options," Nixon said.

"Not if you run it right," Westhead snapped again. He was angry.

"Geez," Nixon said softly.

"This is the offense and it's going to work," said Westhead.

I yawned and shook my head.

Occasionally I'd go out to dinner with a few of the guys, but usually Norm and Michael would come over and we'd fix something. I'm a pretty good cook. I cook hamburgers and chicken mainly. Coop handles the garlic bread—that's his specialty. Norm is our salad man.

Training camp in many respects is like a new school term. In the beginning you're all pepped up and ready to go. Most of the guys are in the gym fifteen to twenty minutes early, shooting around and talking stuff. Everybody is anxious. During practice, if you're on the sidelines waiting to go in, you can't find anyone to take a blow.

"You want a break," I might say to Coop as he races by.

Coop shakes his head.

"Silk, I'm in for you."

"Later," he says.

After a week of two-a-days, though, it's a different story. Everybody is dragging. You won't find a soul in the gym until the coach blows his whistle at ten on the button. Nobody shoots around before practice anymore. And during drills and controlled scrimmages, players are looking over their shoulders for replacements. But none are to be found.

I was bruised and battered by the second week, but I felt good. I was playing well and the left knee was fine. No swelling, no pain. More important, I wasn't even thinking about it anymore. When I rejoined the team last season, I was telling everybody my knee was 95 percent. It wasn't. It was maybe 80 percent. I could never tell myself, "Go in there and get that rebound" or "Grab that loose ball." I never really trusted it, and I can't play that way. I have to be strong and reckless. To play up to the high standards I set for myself, I must concentrate fully on what is happening at the moment. I can't be distracted—and the knee was a distraction.

Actually, I didn't overcome the knee injury until the summer. I was playing a full-court pickup game at the IM (Intramural) Building at Michigan State. I came down with an offensive rebound and tried to take it right back up against these two young guys. I didn't know them, only that they had just graduated from high school and would be entering college in the fall. As I shot, one of them came around from the other side of the hoop and knocked the ball into the stands.

You would have thought Darryl Dawkins had ripped down the basket with his teeth. There were a lot of people watching, and I could hear the murmurs.

"Whoaaa . . ."

"Did you see that?"

"Magic Who?"

The two young men went absolutely wild. They were smacking palms and raising their fists.

"Did I?" said the one who blocked the shot.

"You did," said the other.

"Did I?"

"You did."

Smack. Their palms collided. I didn't say anything, but my temperature rolled up as I went back downcourt. I was burned because the shot was goaltended and they didn't call it. In another situation I might have called it, but I couldn't then. I was being challenged, like Matt Dillon. Some young gunslinger is always calling out the top gun. If you're the top gun and you're called out, you have no choice but to go.

The next time I got the ball, I was away from the hoop maybe twenty feet. The one who goaltended my shot was guarding, but he stood several steps away. He wanted me to pass or, even better, take the jump shot, because that would have been a victory for him. He knew I had to take it to the hoop. Meanwhile, his friend was laying for me on the weak side. I had no option. I had to take it down the pike, which I did. I split them as I went for the basket. They hit me hard and sent me sprawling to the floor but not before I jammed on both of them. I bounced right back up and didn't say a word. Nobody else did, either. The gym turned silent, and in the silence I let out a little yell inside of me, not because I beat the two young boys—I knew I would—but because I realized for the first time that my knee was finally well.

The day we broke camp, Westhead also broke some news. He cut Harvey Knuckles and Bob Elliott, a veteran center we had obtained on a trial basis from the New Jersey Nets two days into camp. It's tough when guys go. You get close to somebody and then—bam!—he's gone. It hurts, and you never know what to say. All you can do is accept it and go on.

After playing against the same people for ten straight days, it was a pleasure to play another team. Training camp eventually turns into a tug-of-war because everybody is running the same play. We beat Seattle in overtime in Fresno to open the preseason and then returned to Los Angeles to play Boston, the world champions, the next night.

What preseason? It was like a playoff game. Westhead, who has a reputation for mainly sticking with his top players, a nucleus of seven or eight men, played for the win. You always play for the win, but preseason is also supposed to be a testing ground for new players and new ideas. Games don't count, but we played the Boston game as if the entire season was riding on its outcome. The starters—me, Norm, Silk, Kareem, and Mitch Kupchak—plus our top reserves—Coop and Mark Landsberger—played most of the game. Boston coach Bill Fitch experimented during the first half and fell so far behind that he had to go with his starters the second half to make the score respectable. We won by nine points, but it wore us out.

That game set the tone for the rest of the preseason. The starters averaged nearly as many minutes as they normally would in games that count. We thought it was strange and started talking about it. But nobody said anything to Westhead. We figured he must know what he's doing. Along the way, he traded Butch Carter to Indiana for a draft choice and cut Clay Johnson and Alan Hardy.

Under those circumstances, we did not have much trouble against the opposition. We won six of seven games, with two of those wins coming against the Detroit Pistons, one in the Silverdome in Pontiac, Michigan, and the other in Jenison Field House at Michigan State in Lansing.

Lansing. Back home. It was the first game I'd played before my home fans since turning pro. At the morning shoot-around, I was excited but loose. At one point my mind was wandering and I accidentally made the wrong cut while running a play. At about the time I realized my mistake, I heard this gruff voice from the sidelines: "He never would've done that at Michigan State."

I turned around and started laughing. Standing there was Jud Heathcote, my college coach. The rest of the players burst out laughing. Norman was yelling, "Brainstorm, brainstorm," which is what we call it when somebody gets confused and messes up a play.

That night I had goose bumps. The old field house was sold out. I had bought five hundred tickets and donated them to various boys' clubs in Lansing. Plus, I had to take care of family and friends. People were carrying signs that read MAGIC, WE LOVE YOU, ... IT'S NICE TO HAVE YOU BACK, ... THANKS FOR THE MEMORIES. ... And I was so happy for the way they welcomed the Lakers—Kareem, Jamaal, Norm, Coop, and the others. These guys in Lansing; I don't think the fans ever thought it would happen.

Then they announced the starting lineup, and the place erupted. I thought bricks were going to pop out of the walls. I never heard so much noise in all my life.

And now, on opening day of the regular season, I can't get those cheers out of my mind. I want to hear cheers like that again—in Los Angeles, at the end of the final game of the final round of the NBA Championship playoffs. I want to hear the fans in my new home, Los Angeles, as happy as those in my other home, Lansing, the town that shaped my life.

2

Growing Up

One afternoon during my stay in Lansing for the preseason game, I borrowed Tuck's Jeep and drove through my old neighborhood in the heart of town. The stillness surprised me. I remembered the neighborhood jumping from morning till night. I remembered children swarming all over the streets playing football, kickball, and hide-and-seek. I remembered children tugging and teasing, shouting and whining, laughing and crying. The neighborhood was still only late at night, when the children slept.

It was a lower-middle-class area. The majority of people worked, the men mostly in the automobile and construction industries. They made enough money to cover the mortgages on the simple two-story houses, make the payments on their cars, and support their large families. There were few frills. A bicycle, for example, was a rarity. The one my father bought me went unused because there was never anyone for me to ride with.

Revisiting the neighborhood in Tuck's Jeep, I parked in front of the yellow frame house on Middle Street. My parents, who still owned it, moved in 1979 to a new house I bought with money from my first NBA contract. Parked at the top of the driveway was the old truck my father used for hauling rubbish. There was a fresh coat of paint on the outside of the old house. It looked pretty enough to sell. But inside, my goodness, I could not believe how small it was. The house was empty of furniture, and as I went from room to room, the same thought kept striking me: How did we all live here? I had always pictured it as a big house: a living room, dining room, and a kitchen downstairs; three bedrooms and one bath upstairs; and a basement.

Nine of us, sometimes ten, lived there. My mother and father had the big bedroom. Quincy, Larry, and I had another, and the four girls, Lily Pearl, Kim, and the twins, Evelyn and Yvonne, shared the third. Until we got bunk beds, I slept in the same bed with Larry, who was older by a year. Michael, the oldest of three children my father had before marrying my mother, lived with us part of the time.

Being close in age—I was the fourth of seven—we had our shouting matches and little fights and tantrums. But overall we tolerated each other in the worst of times and enjoyed ourselves in the best. Which in retrospect was affirmation of the strength, wisdom, character, and resourcefulness of my mother, Christine. Out of necessity, she was the family disciplinarian. My father, Earvin Sr., worked at two full-time jobs for nineteen years to keep the family going—a remarkable sacrifice that I didn't fully appreciate until I was older. The only prolonged periods of contact I had with him came on weekends. That's when we watched NBA games on television. He loved basketball. He'd played in high school and had developed a keen understanding and perception of the game's subtleties that he enjoyed sharing with me on those Sundays long ago. His passion became my passion.

Fisher Body was my father's principal employer. He started off there working the grinding boot on the assembly line making Oldsmobile bodies. Working the grinding boot— essentially, smoothing down the metal—was dangerous. Some nights he came home with his shirt burned up and his skin scorched. Once he built up seniority, he transferred out of there and became an intermediate relief man, which is the job he has today.

At first he pumped gas as a second job. He did that seven hours a day for two and a half years, until he couldn't take it any longer. He borrowed some money to buy that truck in the driveway and went into business for himself cleaning up shops and hauling rubbish. He held that job until the family made him quit a couple of years ago.

During those years, he worked a full shift at Fisher Body from four in the afternoon until one the next morning, then cleaned the shops for a couple of hours before going home to sleep. By nine in the morning, he returned to the shops to pick up rubbish to haul to the dump. When he finished, he had maybe two or three hours to rest before punching in at Fisher Body.

"I'd like to say it was like death," he told me once, "but I've never seen death, so maybe it was worse."

But two incomes weren't enough. When the twins were old enough, my mother took a full-time job as a school custodian, which, in essence, gave her a second full-time job. She still had to deal with the kids, dinner, and cleaning house. I came home from school once and saw her sitting at the dining-room table, her eyes closed and her chin resting in the palm of her hand. I was in junior high at the time. She heard me and looked up and smiled a thin smile.

"Mother," I said, "you're really tired, aren't you?"

"Yes, Junior, I am."

"Well, someday I'm going to become somebody and you won't ever have to work again."

She reached for my hand and grasped it. "Oh, thank you, honey," she said with a big smile. "That will be nice."

People talk about my smile, but hers is the original. It is as bright and warm as the sun at midday, and just seeing it perks me up. Seeing her frown, on the other hand, breaks my heart.

Middle Street, in those days, was appropriately named. Its residents were religious, hardworking, clean-living blacks lured to Lansing by the automobile industry and its need for laborers during the boom years of the 1950s and 1960s. One of those who migrated from the South was my father.

He was born in Wesson, Mississippi, and raised on a sharecropper's farm. "At the time I always thought we got half of what we produced for working the land," he says. "That's how it was supposed to work. But looking back, I realized we never got what we earned." His mother left his father and took him to Chicago in 1942, when he was seven years old. But it didn't work out the way she planned it, and she sent him back to Mississippi to live with his grandparents. He rejoined his mother in Chicago seven years later, then returned to Mississippi again to live with his father. He left home for good at nineteen and headed straight for Chicago, where he drifted while looking for permanent work. The search ended with Fisher Body in Lansing, but within a year he was drafted into the U.S. Army. While in the Army he met and married my mother.

Like my father, she was born and raised in the South, her hometown being Tarboro, North Carolina, a rural community in the middle of tobacco country. She loved it there and still cherishes childhood memories of the beautiful countryside, clean air, and a less hectic life. Although her family of ten children was poor, she paints a pretty picture of the rural South and always told us one of her greatest disappointments was that her children were unable to experience country life.

"Country people were so friendly," she'd tell us. "If you saw a neighbor, you'd go right up and say, 'Good morning, how are you?' Not like it is in most big cities, where nobody says anything to anybody. They were help people. If you needed something, your neighbors would all pitch in.

"I can remember as a little girl how the whole family would go over to the ball field and watch the baseball games. My daddy played second base and outfield. He was a big star. All the families came out. It was a big party, and they'd set up these big old barrels of lemonade for all the kids. Yep, you kids today don't know what you missed."

My mother's cousin, an Army buddy of my father's, invited him to Tarboro one weekend and introduced him to my mother. My father was tall, skinny, and, above all, shy. "He looked so lonesome standing there by himself," my mother once told me. "I felt sorry for him, so I asked him how he was doing and things like that. We talked for a few minutes and then I left." They had a lengthier conversation the next time and began dating. They got married while my father still had eleven months to serve in the Army.

When his tour ended, my father reclaimed his job at Fisher Body. He and Mom settled down in the bottom half of a duplex on Logan Street, the main street in Lansing. They bought the house on Middle Street several years later.

Both my parents are religious; my father is a Baptist and my mother, who was a Baptist too, converted and became a Seventh Day Adventist. She made sure I and my brothers and sisters were active in the church, as ushers and as members of the choir. When I was a kid I went to church all the time.

With the kids, my mother handled the day-to-day traumas of family life. She arbitrated arguments over bathroom rights, gave out the punishments for missed chores, and generally kept seven children in line. But the heavy stuff went through my father. Big E, as we called him, wore the pants, and because he worked so hard, the last thing we dared do was make him mad. We always knew it was time to cool it when my mother reached the point of frustration and threatened to bring in Big E.

None of us presented any serious disciplinary problems: no drugs, no major fights, and no incidents requiring police intervention. During the years I grew up, Lansing seemed relatively wholesome and peaceful.

The one time Big E got a call to take care of me was the day I got caught stealing candy and balloons from a neighborhood store. I was nine at the time and going to Main Street School. My friends and I were feeling our oats, and we decided stealing would be an adequate test of courage. Being the leader, I volunteered to do it. The lady behind the counter knew me and my family. Through the mirrors in the corners of the store, she saw that my hands were not quicker than her eyes. I strolled out of there, thinking I had pulled it off. I learned otherwise as soon as I stepped inside the front door of my house. The lady had called.

My mother yelled and sent me upstairs to wait for my father. It was Saturday, so I knew he'd be home soon. My heart pounded, really thumped, as I heard him come in the front door and begin walking up the stairs. I cried as he opened the door to my room. Without saying a word, he took off his strap, put me over his knee, and whipped me good a couple of times. I wailed like a baby, more from the crime than the punishment, which really didn't hurt that much. When he had finished, he pulled up a chair and faced me. I continued to sob away.

"Why'd you do it, Junior?" he asked.

"I don't know. I was showing off to my friends, and the next thing I knew I was doing it."

"That's pretty dumb."

I nodded and sniffled some more.

"Listen, Junior, you don't have to steal. If you want something, tell me. I'll get it for you. If I can't, then you know you can do without it. Understand?"

I nodded and sniffled again.

"You don't have to be stealing. That'll only get you into trouble and you're too smart for that. Okay?"

"Okay," I said, trying to pull myself together.

He stood up and gently shook my head.

"C'mon," he said. "Get dressed. Let's go out to the race-track."

He loved the dragsters and took me out to the track about twenty miles outside of town almost every weekend. Usually just the two of us went because the older boys were into their own things and the girls weren't interested.

I cherished those evenings. He and I would point and shout and jump up and down as those cars whipped down the strip doing more than two hundred miles an hour over a quarter-mile. We ate hot dogs and talked the whole time. And when it was over, I'd fall asleep with my head in his lap on the way home. On this particular night, I forgot what had transpired during the day and fell asleep as soon as I hit the pillow. My father never mentioned the incident again; he didn't have to.

About the time I began playing organized basketball, I started growing vertically instead of horizontally. That was the end of my first nickname, June Bug. My father had called me that because, as he said, I was stout.

The Lansing elementary schools played organized games at each grade level, beginning with the third. They were played at various high schools every Saturday. On one of those Saturdays, my school, Main Street, played Holmes Street, a school that had a big, chubby kid named Jay Vincent. We didn't meet then, but within a few years we came to know each other well, as rivals through junior high and high school, then as teammates at Michigan State, and again as rivals in the NBA.

It was impossible to distinguish one player from another in third grade because nobody knew what he was doing and coaches shuffled entire units in and out of the game at once.

It was so hectic that a team would often wind up with ten players on the court. So it wasn't until the fourth and fifth grades, when games began to take on form and meaning, that I began to realize how much better I was than everybody else my age. I also discovered how much I loved to win.

In the fifth grade I learned that basketball could also cause me suffering. All week I was psyched for the fifth-grade championship game against Michigan Avenue School. I couldn't wait for Saturday. I even had these fantastic dream sequences every night, all of which ended in victory. But a couple of days before the game, Greta Dart, my teacher, punished me for failing to turn in an assignment.

"Earvin," she said, "you can't play basketball Saturday."

"But this is for the championship," I pleaded.

She didn't care. I had messed up and she was making me pay for it. Even my mother refused to intervene. On Saturday I watched the game from the sidelines—as the coach. I was proud of the guys. They were outmanned terribly but played hard and lost only because of a bad call at the buzzer.

I couldn't stay mad at Mrs. Dart very long. She and my mother developed a strong friendship, and her husband, Jim, who loved kids, later coached our school teams and took me under his wing as his star pupil. I eventually adopted them as my godparents.

Mrs. Dart and I still argue about that old punishment whenever we get together. She insists she did the right thing and I say she overreacted, that she never understood that the game was proportionately more important to my development than the missed assignment. If my mother is present, she supports Mrs. Dart. "You have to stick by your principles," my mother always says.

My mother once did the same thing to my sister Evelyn, a pretty good player in her own right who later won a basketball scholarship to the University of South Carolina. Evelyn came home with a subpar report card once and—boom!— her basketball was gone. "I told her what I was going to do if it happened," my mother explained at the time, "and now I have to do it." My mother was always consistent. If she said she was going to do something, she did it. She didn't make promises she couldn't keep, just as she didn't make threats she had no intention of carrying out.

While Mom was pleased with my basketball, there were many times she would have preferred I had another passion. She was always yelling at me to stop bouncing the basketball in the house and became absolutely irate over ball prints on the walls. But I think the socks got to her more than anything else, even more than the cold dinners and the chores I sometimes forgot because I was in such a hurry to get to the courts.

I played basketball in the living room when my parents weren't around. Sometimes I'd play with Larry or Evelyn, other times alone. I'd mark a rectangle on opposite walls for baskets and use balled-up socks for the ball. The object was to hit the rectangle with the socks. The hoops, drawn in pencil, erased easily enough, but it seemed that the socks always turned up missing when my mother was dressing the twins for school.

"Junior," she'd scream. "What did you do with the twins' socks?"

"I put 'em back, Mom," I'd yell back.

But they were never where they were supposed to be. Weeks later they would turn up, stashed inside the sofa or buried beneath chairs.

I don't think she seriously regarded basketball as a potential career for me until I went to Michigan State on scholarship. She hoped I'd become a minister because she always wanted a minister in the house, but thought I'd become a singer because my friends and I always got together on summer nights to sing on street corners. She liked my voice and put me in the children's choir at church. I even played bass guitar for a while. I loved music, but not like I loved basketball.

I spent so much time on the Main Street courts that I could have had my mail delivered there. During the school year I would get up early in the morning, long before I had to, and practice before breakfast. The school was two blocks from my house, on the corner of Main and West streets. It had four outdoor courts surrounded by a waist-high fence. Everybody who ever ran into that fence or had to scale it in pursuit of a ball bouncing into the street cursed it to death. Main Street was my home turf, the place where I became a player and beat all comers. I also set fashion trends there by wearing red Chucks—short for Converse Chuck Taylor All-Stars—and multicolored shoelaces. In summer, I played from morning until night. In winter, I shoveled the snow right off the court. Nothing stopped me from playing. I always had a basketball in my hands or one nearby. It was my girl, and I treated it right.

My regular partners in those days were Wayne, Dino, and James. We played two-on-two until we got tired, then P-I-G, H-O-R-S-E, or a game we invented called Yo Mama. It was a talking game where the shooter had to match a shot while the other guys talked about his mama. If I was shooting, they would yell, "Yo Mama's Christine Crackers. You want some crumbs, boy?" Wayne's mother was named Lee, so we would call out, "General Lee. Shoot down, General Lee." Dino's mother was Catherine. We called her Cat Woman. It was Cat this, Cat that. "You want some Purina, Cat Child?" With James it was "Party at Claire's" which was the name of his mother as well as the street we used to go to to party. It was all in fun, but games sometimes heated up because nobody liked the idea of his mother being made fun of.

While Big E never pushed basketball on me or pushed anything on any of us, he encouraged me when he realized the interest was genuine. He coached me on a few things and occasionally took me on the court for a little one-on-one. He had tricks, but they didn't work once I passed him for good in the ninth grade. He recognized my talent early. By the sixth grade I was much bigger than kids my age, a good ball handler, and an expert shooter. I stood six-even when I started Dwight Rich Junior High, six foot four the next year, and six-five as a ninth grader.

I was at Dwight Rich the first time my name appeared in print. A friend brought the paper to show me and there it was: "Earvin Johnson scored 26 points to lead Rich Junior High to victory." My eyes popped out. "Man, oh man," I yelled. "Look it here. I didn't know they were going to do this." I jumped up and down and ran downstairs to show my mother. She smiled and said, "That's nice, Junior."

From that point on, my reputation spread to every school and playground in the city. Players came from across town to play at Main Street, and I reciprocated by visiting their courts. My rivalry with Jay Vincent, which had gotten under way by this time, heated up. Jay lived on the east side of Lansing; I lived on the west. He was top gun in his neighborhood; I was top in mine. We were the same age, the same size, and, in the eyes of some (mostly his friends), of equal ability. We had some wars. We played school against school, and during the summer one-on-one in the Parks and Recreation League. I won just about every game. The only time he ever beat me for a championship was in the ninth grade, the year he really came on as a player. We were very competitive in everything we played, whether it was basketball, football, Ping-Pong, bowling, or pool. We were the best, and because we were the best, a victory over the other was the most important thing in the world. The rivalry became even more intense as we entered high school, Jay at Eastern and me at Everett.

Through it all, I tried to contain my ego, and I believe I succeeded. My fame and popularity increased disproportionately to my age and emotional growth. It became com-

monplace for strangers to stop me on the street while I was
still a junior-high-school student to tell me how great I was.
I appreciated the thought and thanked them politely. But I
shrugged off the praise because of a deep-rooted reluctance
to believe it. I knew I was good—that was obvious. But how
good? Never good enough, I thought. It was probably that
basic insecurity that drove me on.

Pro ball? That goal was stored deep in the back of my
mind. I used it only as a source for dreams and inspiration. I
rarely talked about it, and when I did, it was only to those
closest to me. Being basically goal-oriented, I set reachable
goals, and when those were reached I set new ones. In
junior high, my goals were first to win the seventh-grade
championship, then the eighth, and then the ninth. Losing
the ninth to Jay was a terrible blow, one I cried over for
weeks. In high school I set new goals: to make the starting
team as a tenth grader, to win the conference championship, and to make All-City.

A chance encounter with Dr. Charles Tucker at the end
of my ninth-grade year helped me focus my goals. Tuck was
a twenty-seven-year-old psychologist for the Lansing School
District. A street-wise, gym-wise black, he had a firm grip
on the community and the game of basketball.

Tuck was born in Mississippi, but at twelve he moved to
Michigan with his parents. He made All-City guard in Kala-
mazoo and Junior College All-American at Kellogg Community College in Battle Creek, Michigan. He then went to
Western Michigan, where he played ball and earned a
master's degree in psychology.

He followed his own basketball dream for several years.
He tried out with Dallas and Kentucky of the ABA, then
caught on with the Memphis Tams for a few games. Later,
right before my senior year of high school, he was one of
the last players cut by the Philadelphia 76ers in 1976 in his
last pro tryout. Through the disappointment, Tuck's love
for the game never diminished. He played in the Continen-

tal League between pro tryouts and led the league in assists three straight seasons. During this same period, he returned to Western Michigan and earned a doctorate in psychology at the age of twenty-five.

"I've always been interested in people," he says when asked about his interest in psychology, "always interested in what's going on in their minds, and how they try to figure things out. I guess it's my way of trying to outthink the other guy and stay a step ahead of the pack. I've always been the type of guy who sits in the background and observes. If I'm unfamiliar with the setting, I won't say much. I'll just wait and watch until I know what's happening."

Tuck's philosophy carries over onto the basketball court. He compensates for a lack of size by outsmarting his opponent. He thinks the game as well as anyone I've ever met. If the man he's playing only goes left, Tuck forces him right, not once in a while, but all the time. If the man can't shoot the jumper, Tuck makes him take it. If the man has a short fuse, Tuck will do anything short of pouring gasoline over his head and lighting a match to ignite it. Tuck plays a pro game, a winning game, and over the years he has imparted much of his considerable knowledge to me.

We first met in class at Rich Junior High. He had an office at Everett and came to counsel a group of the leaders in the graduating class. He talked about the growing responsibility of the individual in society, which held my interest for about a minute and a half. He seemed to be a good dude, but I didn't think any more about him until I saw him again later in the afternoon. He came to the courts and watched a few games. He had gotten rid of his coat and tie and wore sweats and sneakers. When the other kids left the court, he came over.

"You want to go one-on-one?" he asked.

I nodded and tossed him the ball.

"Take it out," I offered.

"I'll shoot," he said.

That was fine with me. "Go ahead, shoot."

He hit a jumper from a distance and took the ball out. This is one cocky dude, I thought to myself. After he backed me down, hooked me around the waist, and scored the first hoop on a short fall-away jumper, I wanted to teach him a lesson. But he did all the teaching. He hooked me, pushed me, tugged my shorts, stepped on my toes, and, if I so much as touched him on the jumper, called a foul and took the ball out. I ran a temperature at first, especially because I didn't like the idea of looking bad in front of my boys, who were watching from the sidelines. But I simmered down and decided to play it cool. I didn't argue. If he called a foul, fine, he took it out. He was good, but I knew I'd get him sometime down the line. And when I got him, it wasn't going to matter how many fouls he called.

"Nice game, Earvin," he said when he finished.

I nodded and didn't say a word. I kept my expression blank. My boys were angry.

"You shouldn't let him do that to you," said one.

"It's cool," I said.

Tuck strolled over. He was wearing this big smile. I wanted to bite it off.

"What's the matter?" he asked.

"Nothin'," I said. "Why?"

"You have to learn how to play the pro game," he said.

"I guess so."

"Let's go again tomorrow."

"I'll be here."

3

Tuck

All through my childhood I counted on going to Sexton
High, my neighborhood high school. I attended Sexton football games, basketball games, pep rallies; I used to go there
to watch the players work out on weekends. The basketball
coach knew me and followed my progress and talked to me
about playing there someday. Sexton had a good reputation
for basketball, and I wanted to contribute to it.

But I never went there. Instead of attending school a half-
mile from home, I was bused out of the neighborhood to
Everett High, a predominantly white school about fifteen
minutes away. Forced busing was in its heyday, and I was
unlucky enough to live just inside its border line in Lansing.
Busing wasn't popular in my parts, especially with me,
because all my friends went to Sexton. My parents didn't
like it, either, but they accepted it in the name of law. I told

them it was a lousy law. I even appealed by letter to the school board, but that didn't do any good.

Quincy and Larry, who were bused to Everett before me, each had unpleasant experiences. In Quincy's time, which were the early days of busing, the whites reacted violently to having blacks in their schools and neighborhoods. They staged protest rallies; there were brick-throwing incidents, near-riots, fights in the school, and instances of overt racism.

Most of that was over by the time Larry enrolled, but some scars remained. Larry was a good basketball player—good enough, I thought, to play for Everett. But George Fox, Everett's coach, didn't think so and cut him from the team, an action that Larry interpreted as racist. In an angry confrontation with Fox, Larry swore he would make sure his kid brother never played for him.

Needless to say, I didn't begin my high school career full of enthusiasm, optimism, and openness. I entered a white environment for the first time looking for something to go wrong, and it didn't take long.

Although Everett wasn't recognized as a basketball power, it had one of its better teams the year before I arrived. It had won the district title and had some good players returning. But Fox knew this team would be different and was prepared to build the program around me. I felt bad that I couldn't redeem Larry's pledge, but what could I do? I had to play basketball somewhere.

If Fox had any doubts about my ability, they were erased that first summer right before I officially enrolled at school. In my first game for Coach Fox in the summer league, I put on a show. Playing forward and center, I took the ball off the boards, drove it downcourt and dunked or made a fancy pass time after time. We led 30–2 at the end of the first eight-minute period. The kids we played against had never seen anything like it before and were hopelessly overmatched. Afterwards, the opposing coach cornered Fox and told him, "George, that kid has got to be one of the greatest basketball players you'll ever see."

When school started, some of the returning players weren't ready for me. They regarded me as a young hotshot who threatened their status on the team. Resentment surfaced in scrimmage on the first day of practice. On three successive plays I got away from my man, broke wide open under the hoop, and never got the ball. The same player, a white senior starter, handled the ball on all three plays. At first I figured he just missed me. The second time I got suspicious. Then the third time, when he completely ignored me and fired up a long jumper, I grabbed the rebound and slammed it to the floor.

"Give it up!" I screamed. "I was wide open three straight times. What the hell's going on here?"

He came at me, pushed me, and yelled racial slurs. Players separated us before I could get to him. I was so mad. Wow!

Fox stepped in and said, "Hey, cut this b.s. out. We've got to be a team."

"If it's going to be like this," I told Fox, "then I want out of here."

"When Earvin's wide open like that, make sure he gets the ball," he told the other guy. Then he turned to me. "Earvin," he said, "you have to learn to be more tolerant of your teammates and not blow your stack if they miss you on a pass."

I couldn't believe it. Was Fox blaming me? My first reaction was, Okay, this is how I get over to Sexton, where I belong. If I complain about racism, the school board has to transfer me.

Tuck ran me down in the locker room after practice. He had been there and knew I didn't start anything. He told me to cool it, that I was jumping to conclusions.

"What're you talking about?" I snapped. "You heard what he called me. I don't have to stand for that."

"I'm telling you to cool down," he said. "It had nothing to
do with race."

"That's what you say."

"Listen. I'm being real about this. You're the best player
out there, right?"

"Yeah," I said.

"You know it, I know it, the coach knows it, all the other
players know it, now don't you think he knows it, too?"

I nodded.

"Damn right, he knows it and he doesn't like it," Tuck
continued. "I wouldn't like it, either, if some young dude
stepped in and took over my team. So he's frustrated, and
he expressed his frustration. That's all it was. It had nothing
to do with the color of your skin. Now, if you're as good as
everybody thinks you are, you'll forget the whole thing and
show up here tomorrow like nothing happened."

"What about Fox jumping on me?"

"This is new to him, too. I'll talk to him."

Fox had his work cut out for him. He knew the game and
how to coach it, but he wasn't prepared for the sudden
success and he didn't know how to deal with the vehicle to
that success—the exceptional black athlete. He was a product of the small-town Midwest: religious, hardworking, honest, a man of will and strong principles. Over the years his
teams usually played .500 ball.

Until my arrival at Everett, neither success nor blacks
had played a part in his modest career. He was a fundamen-
talist who coached out of the book. He cringed and gritted
his teeth whenever he saw a length-of-the-court pass, a no-
look pass, or a behind-the-back pass. He didn't go for all that
"fancy stuff," as he called it. To Fox, it was a crime for a ball
handler to leave his feet before knowing what he was going
to do with the ball, and it was "murder one" if he came
down with it. Fox didn't know what to think about a player
taking the ball off the defensive boards and driving it downcourt the way I did because he had never seen it done

regularly. He also was a firm believer in the chain of command, in which he made and passed on decisions he expected to be implemented immediately. Input from players was rejected outright.

To his credit, Fox opened up his mind. With help from Tuck, his unofficial adviser, he relaxed some of the rigid rules both on and off the court—most important, the lines of communication between the players and himself. He even allowed us to turn up music on our "squawk boxes" in the locker room before games, which was a major concession for him. Previously he'd considered the pregame period a solemn time, one for silence and concentration. The concept that players drew inspiration from the music they played on tape cassettes boggled his mind.

As he responded to us, we responded in kind. Everybody began to understand that once all the petty stuff was cut away, the bottom line was a mutual desire to win. All he really requested was dedication. His saying was, "If you want to be a ball player, you have to work; if you don't, hit the road." He appreciated the fact that I was a good practice player and never put him into the impossible position of having to deal with a double standard.

Fox was anxious for the first season to begin. He knew he had something special and had trouble containing his excitement around his coaching pals. Before the season, he told them, "I got a kid who's going to make believers out of everybody. He's going to be the greatest player you ever saw."

I was equally anxious, maybe too anxious. As a result, I came out tight for the opener and never unwound. One thing for sure, I was nothing to brag about. I had about a dozen points and only a few rebounds and assists. I guess I inadvertently contributed as a decoy, though—by standing around in a stupor all game and wasting the efforts of the man guarding me. We won by one point, and the victory took some of the sting out. But if I felt bad, Fox, who had to face his pals, must have felt worse. "Well, George," said one of them, "I think your expectations are a little too high." But Fox wouldn't back down. "Just wait," he said. "I see the kid every day in practice and I know what he's capable of doing."

I never let Fox down again.

By the middle of the season, I was turning it out on a regular basis and Everett High was receiving recognition as one of the powers in the area. Against Jackson Parkside, I had 36 points, 18 rebounds, and 16 assists. I felt I could fly. After the game, people came by to congratulate me and shake my hand in the locker room. Reporters flocked around me asking questions. I just leaned back and took it all in, enjoying every moment of it. Fred Stabley, Jr., a sportswriter for the *Lansing State Journal*, stood in the back of the pack until the others left. Then he approached me.

"Earvin," he said, "that was some performance out there tonight."

"Thanks," I said.

"I gotta give you a nickname."

"A nickname?" I hoped he wouldn't come up with Junior or June Bug.

"Is that all right?"

"Yeah, I guess so."

"I can't call you Dr. J because that's already taken. I can't call you Big E because that one is taken, too. . . . So, I thought. . . ."

He paused for a moment. I smiled in anticipation.

"What about . . . ?"

He paused again. Then,

"Can I call you Magic?"

The words rushed out like tap water from an open faucet. Then they seemed to hang in the air for a moment. Magic, I thought. Magic. It sounded good.

"Yeah," I said, "okay."

I picked up a copy of the *Lansing State Journal* the next day. It was in print: Earvin "Magic" Johnson.

It looked funny. It embarrassed me at first, but the more I looked at it, the more I liked it. Magic. Yes, it had a nice ring to it.

The next time we met, Stabley asked me what I thought of the nickname. I was still a little embarrassed, but I told him it was all right, and he continued using it. Soon after, other writers picked up on it, then the fans. One purpose the nickname served was to single me out as a target for opposing fans and players, a challenge I gladly accepted.

"Who is this Magic dude?" I heard one guy say in the stands before one of our games. I was sitting with my teammates, watching the Junior Varsity game. The voice came from behind us. Then another voice said, "He's the dude down there. The big one." "Well," said the first, "he don't look so tough." Whoever it was who said that found out differently.

With the exception of my mother, members of the family accepted the name in stride. My father's initial reservation that a name like Magic might be too much to live up to faded as he grew to like it.

"You have to be careful," he warned me one day. We were in the living room, watching an NBA game on television. "By naming you Magic, people will get the idea you can actually perform magic. No matter what happens, or how badly your team is losing, they will expect you to do something to make it better."

"Don't worry," I said. "It's only a nickname."

"Do you like it?"

"I think so."

"I'm glad of that, because you're the one who has to live with it."

As a regular churchgoer and deeply religious woman, my mother disapproved of the nickname because the concept of magic contradicted her belief. She insisted my God-given gifts had nothing at all to do with magic. I agreed, and tried to convince her that it was only a nickname, nothing real deep. But in time, of course, there were those who did confuse reality with illusion and believed the magic was real. Who knows? Maybe they were right.

It didn't seem to affect my teammates. They continued calling me Earvin, or E.J., or E, and so did Fox. We had our names stitched to the backs of our warm-ups and "E. Johnson" remained stitched to mine. But as the season wore on, more and more fans and more and more sportswriters and broadcasters began calling me Magic. Within a few years, it became so widely accepted that many people assumed Magic Johnson was my given name. It was not unusual for me to go to an airline-ticket counter, for example, and hear the clerk, after scanning the computer screen, glumly say, "I'm sorry, Mr. Johnson, we don't have a reservation for you. We have an E. Johnson, but no M. Johnson."

We cruised through most of the first season, usually winning by ten to fifteen points, but also winning some by blowouts. Including me, we started two sophomores, plus a junior and two seniors. The sixth man was another tenth grader. The junior was Reggie Chastine, a five-foot-three-inch guard who became my best friend and constant companion. We made quite a sight around school, he at five-three, me at six-five; Mutt and Jeff, they called us. He eased me into the social circles, which accelerated my adjustment to the new environment. By the middle of the year I no longer had any desire to transfer to Sexton. Everett was home, and I became very active in clubs and activities. I joined the school newspaper, *The Viking*, as a reporter and eventually became head of advertising.

Reggie and I used to check out the girls in the stands during time-outs, trying to decide which ones we wanted to date that night. After making our picks, we'd send the team manager over to make contact. Yes, I adapted well at Everett.

We finished with a 22–2 record, losing only to Detroit Northeastern during the season and a crusher to Dearborn

Fordson in the state quarterfinals. We led Fordson by thirteen points entering the final quarter and blew five one-and-ones from the free-throw line during the last few minutes. Two of those one-and-ones belonged to me. I broke down and cried when it was over. Losing shorts out my emotional circuitry. I learned to control my emotions better as I grew older, but as a tenth grader they were still fragile. I was helpless in defeat.

It was about this time that my bond with Dr. Tucker tightened. He took me everywhere—to the IM Building at Michigan State, to the playgrounds in Detroit, to his summer basketball camp, and, best of all, to Detroit, Chicago, and Indianapolis to watch the pros. He seemed to know everybody, and he somehow always got us into the locker rooms after games, where he'd introduce me to some of the players. I tried to be so cool, like the first time I met Kareem. The Lakers had just beaten the Pistons in Cobo Arena in Detroit. The locker room was crowded, and I self-consciously stood alone by the door. I knew I wasn't supposed to be in there. All the while I watched Tuck mill around as he usually did. Suddenly he turned towards me and beckoned with a wave of the hand. I shook my head. He gestured more urgently. I knew he meant business. I walked over. As soon as I was within reach, he grabbed me and jerked me in front of Kareem, who was in a hurry and dressing quickly.

"Kareem," said Tuck, "I'd like you to meet Earvin Johnson."

Kareem put out his hand and I shook it.

"It's nice to meet you, Earvin," he said.

I was awestruck, and, for some reason, I said, "Thanks, Kareem."

On the ride home I was still excited.

"Tuck," I said, "I don't know how to thank you. Kareem Abdul-Jabbar. I can't believe it. Kareem."

I put out my right hand, pulled up my jacket sleeve, and

looked it over. "With this hand, the Big Fella. I can't wait until tomorrow morning to tell my boys."

I could see a smile cross Tuck's face in the light cast by an oncoming truck.

"You just take care of yourself," he said. "Work real hard and don't let anything come between you and winning, and someday some kid will shake your hand and brag to his partners about it."

"You really think so?"

"Yep." He nodded. "And keep your head on. That's the hardest part."

Tuck and I were attracted to each other from the beginning. To me, he was a tough player who knew the ins and outs of the game I loved. To Tuck, I guess in some respects, I represented the player he would never be. Whatever the reason, we hit it off. We played one-on-one almost daily and never for the fun of it. I wanted to beat him badly, but it took time.

"You cheat," I'd say to him in disgust and exasperation after being called for a foul.

"Right," he'd respond as he put the ball in bounds. "Nine–two, I'm up."

He taught me how to use my hands, my elbows, how to fake a foul. He pounded into me the importance of putting the shot up the moment a foul was committed in order to get to the free-throw line, where, he said, games were won. He taught the pro game, that one had to play with the head as well as the body. I soaked up Tuck's knowledge.

From the ninth grade on, I made it a point to play against older and better players. By playing against the same guys every day, particularly if you're beating them to death, you develop a false sense of security that stagnates your growth as a player. I kept searching for better competition and eventually started hanging out at the IM Building, where the Michigan State players worked out during the off-season. At first I was content to sit against the wall and watch, studying moves and techniques that I'd play over and over again in my mind at night. When I summoned enough courage, I began shooting by myself on the side baskets; I'd shoot and watch all day long. I stayed at that stage for a while. But eventually I noticed that some of the players kept an eye on me. One of them was Terry Furlow, a jump-shot artist who was the Michigan State star at the time.

One Saturday I arrived early. As I headed for my side basket, I noticed only seven players on the floor. They seemed to be waiting for an eighth so they could play their usual game of four-on-four full court. Five minutes passed, then ten. They continued shooting. So did I. We were the only ones in the gym. After another five minutes, Furlow walked over to my basket and looked me over from head to toe.

"Hey, boy," he said.

"Me?" I said, pointing a finger to my chest.

He rolled his eyes at the response and shook his head. "What grade you in?"

"Ninth."

"Ninth?" he repeated in dismay. "Can you play or what?"

"Yeah," I said. "I can play."

"C'mon, then."

I was nervous. I had never played against this kind of talent. Furlow was incredible, firing in long-distance jumpers right in his man's face. I didn't take a shot the first game, concentrating solely on playing good defense, making the good pass, hitting the boards. After a few games, I began to loosen up and take more initiative on offense. I shot the jumper and drove the middle, but all the while I avoided anything fancy, like dunking in somebody's face. I wasn't about to show off against those dudes. Before the day was out, I felt they had accepted me. They banged me, pushed, and slapped away at my arms, but I hung in there.

As I entered the gym the next day, they were choosing up

sides. Furlow saw me coming. "Here comes the young boy," he said. "Better get him." From then on I played regularly with them. Terry, Benny White, and Lindsay Hairston took me in, treating me like a kid brother and taking me to the dorm to hang out after workouts. Lindsay, the center, often picked me up at my house and drove me to campus to show me around.

Terry liked to show me off to his friends, introducing me as his "young boy." "This is my boy here," he'd say. "He's going to turn out and be something." He came to most of my high school games, always making a grand entrance, decked out in his finest clothes, a beautiful girl on each arm, and his entourage dutifully following in his wake. He'd take the whole front row. Yep, I was his boy, all right. At his parties, he'd literally stop the music when I'd arrive.

"This is Fur-low," he'd announce. He liked the effect of a slight pause between the syllables. "Turn on the lights."

The lights would immediately be turned on.

"C'mon over here," he'd say, while grabbing me by the neck. "Look around. You see anything you like? Whatever you see, it's on me."

The place would be filled with girls, and they'd all be looking over at me and smiling. I'd get so embarrassed I'd start laughing. Furlow would smile and let me go.

"You're on your own, boy," he'd say. Then he'd call out, "Put the music back on and turn down the lights."

He was crazy but super nice. He ran the show on court, too. He liked taking me one-on-one, usually beating me easily by scores of 15–5, 15–7, something like that.

"C'mon out here, young boy," he'd challenge. I had to go; you can never turn down a challenge. He'd take the ball out. "Take this with you," he'd say. Swish, from twenty-five feet. He was Mr. IM, he and Tuck.

Furlow had a chance to be something himself. He was a first-round draft choice of the Philadelphia 76ers in 1976 and played four years in the NBA before being killed in an auto accident during the spring of 1980. He was one shooting rascal, but teams steered clear of him once word got around the league that he was into drugs. Traces of drugs found in the car after his death didn't help whatever was left of his reputation. I never understood the drugs. I asked him many times why he took them, but he always shrugged me off, usually with a joke or wisecrack. He never pushed drugs on me or anybody else. That wasn't his style. What he did, he did for—and to—himself. But he also did everything he possibly could for his mother in Flint, Michigan. I loved him for that.

I first played against George Gervin during the summer between my tenth and eleventh grades. He put some stuff on me—whoosh!—that had my head spinning every which way. He had moves I'd never seen before, all sorts of little spins and finger rolls. He'd put the ball in your face, then finger-roll it up. After a while I just stopped, hands on hips, and stood in awe for a moment. "How are you supposed to stop him?" I asked, not really expecting an answer. Ice, cool as ever, gave me a hint of a smile.

In time, Tuck's influence, which I welcomed, increased, but never to the point of taking advantage of me or usurping the authority of my father. If anything, he stimulated my father's interest in my career. Even before meeting my parents, which he didn't do for more than a year, he made sure I told them who I was with and where I was going.

"Did you tell your dad?" he'd ask as soon as I jumped into the car to go watch a pro game in Detroit.

"No, it's all right."

"No, it isn't all right. You go in there and tell him where you're going."

"My dad doesn't care."

"Yes, he does."

So I'd get out of the car, slam the door, and go back in the house to tell my father I was going with Tuck to Detroit to see the Pistons. He'd rarely say anything, just nod.

"I told you he doesn't care," I'd say to Tuck back in the car.

"He cares."

Much later I learned my father didn't intervene in my friendship with Tuck because he was always kept informed.

Another time, we were returning from Indianapolis. My partner, Reggie Chastine, was along. It was late. Earlier, Reggie and I had arranged a late-night rendezvous with a couple of Lansing girls. While stopping for hamburgers halfway home, I called to tell the girls that Reggie and I were on our way. I winked to Reggie as I sat down at the table. Tuck looked at both of us. He knew something was going on.

"I'll drop Reggie off first," Tuck said as we entered Lansing.

"No, that's all right," I said. "Drop us off together."

Tuck kept driving. By this time it was two in the morning and the winter streets were cold and deserted. I tried to stop Tuck about two blocks from my house.

"This is good right here, Tuck. You can let us off."

"Nope," he said. "It's too cold out. I'll drop you off at the house."

Tuck pulled up to the curb in front of my house, and I got out.

"I'll holler for you tomorrow," I told him.

"Thanks, Tuck," Reggie said while climbing out of the back seat.

Reggie and I took a couple of slow steps towards the house while waiting for Tuck to drive off. I didn't hear anything, so I turned around. Tuck sat behind the wheel, watching. I walked back and leaned my head through the window.

"Bye," I said.

"You go straight into that house," he said. He had his adult voice on.

"It's all right."

"You go in that house, wake your mother up, and tell her you're back. After that you can do whatever you want."

I stormed away. Man, I was so mad. Reggie and I went into the house, and that was the end of our evening. There was no way my mother was about to let us out of the house at that hour. I didn't talk to Tuck for a week.

Eventually Tuck and my father sought each other out and became close friends. Each was born in Mississippi, each was honest, open, and high-principled, each loved basketball, and each had my best interests at heart. They made it almost impossible for me to mess up. Tuck, only ten years younger than my father, frequently functioned as the intermediary because of my father's work hours. The two of them often got together at my father's night job and discussed what was happening in my life.

"Most kids don't want their parents around because they're ashamed of some of the stuff going on," says Tuck, the psychologist. "They don't think their parents know or understand anything. That's the worst mistake a kid can make. First of all, parents instinctively know when something's up, and secondly, they understand more often than not.

"You should always keep them informed and involved in your life. I'm not saying they should make all the decisions. They may not be qualified in certain areas, but they will appreciate the gesture and allow everything to run more smoothly. Besides, your parents are the ones who really care about you, more so than the agents, lawyers, team owners, and coaches."

All through high school my clashes with Jay Vincent stirred the juices of local fans. When we were tenth graders, the interest was so great that the game was moved from Eastern, Jay's school, to another school to accommodate an additional one thousand fans. Eastern's new gym, ready for the next season, held 5,000, but it still wasn't large enough for one game our senior year.

One summer day Jay and I ran into each other at an outdoor concert at Hunters Park. He was with his boys, and I was with mine. We talked and jived and swayed to the music. We both wore our Chucks just in case we ran into a game. During intermission we wandered over to the basketball court down the hill from the stage and checked out a game being played by some guys who had been local stars a few years earlier.

After the game, one of the winners pointed to us and said, "Get both of 'em. We want Vincent and Johnson."

Jay looked at me; I looked at Jay. We smiled.

"Let's go out there and wear those boys out," I said.

It was the Jay Vincent–Earvin Johnson Show. He came down, wham! I came down, wham! Soon almost the entire concert crowd jammed around the court or lined the hill to watch Jay and me do our things. It seemed like there must have been a couple of thousand people, few of whom left when the band returned from its break.

We warmed up those nets and gave the people something to talk about for months. From that day on, the players prohibited Jay and me from ever playing on the same team.

By the start of my junior year, I had grown another inch to reach six foot six and had gained ten pounds. I made All-City and second-team All-State as a tenth grader. But what I wanted most was the state championship we let slip away.

Everett started the season ranked in the Top Ten. Because of my ball handling, Fox moved me to guard and played me at point on the 1–3–1 offense, giving me more flexibility and freedom than ever. We had another great year, losing only once during the regular season. But again we were disappointed in the state tournament. We led Detroit's Catholic Central in the semifinals by five at the half and blew it in the second. This one was my fault all the way. Instead of asserting myself and taking it to the hoop as opportunities presented themselves, I repeatedly passed off in a conscious attempt to get everybody on the team involved.

This loss hurt even more than the one the year before. At school the next day everybody complained about how we blew it, and how we would have won had we done this and that. Just about everybody told me I passed too much. I couldn't take it. Just talking about it upset me, so I called home.

"Momma," I said, "come get me."

"Come get you?" she asked. She was getting ready to go to work. "What for? Are you sick?"

"No."

"Then what's the matter?"

"Everybody's going on about the game and talking about what went wrong. I just can't take it."

"Honey," she said, "when you played, did you play your best?"

"Yes."

"You gave it everything you had?"

"Yes."

"Now, why are you upset? You say you want to play pro ball, right?"

"Yes."

"Well, you're not going to win all your games in the pros. Are you going to get upset and walk away every time you lose a game?"

"No."

"Then you go back to class and think about it. If somebody tells you what you should have done, you tell him he had the same chance as you to play and if he could have done it better he should have been the one out there. Okay?"

"All right."

A loss that hurt much more came a little bit later. It was the death of Reggie Chastine in an automobile accident during the summer following my junior year. Reggie had gone to visit his girl friend in Jackson, Michigan. There, another car ran a stop sign and collided with Reggie's car.

I didn't know the seriousness of the injuries when I first heard about the accident that evening. All night I tossed and turned with worry. Then, about 6:30 in the morning, his brother called to tell me Reggie was dead. I couldn't believe it. I left my house and started running, just running down the streets. I had no idea where or how long I ran. I just kept running, past stop signs, through red lights, over lawns, down alleys. Running and crying.

I thought about the times we'd spent together, the fun we'd had, the love I felt for him, and the emptiness that already had begun to grow in my heart. We had some outrageous times, mostly innocent stuff but not always. Once Reggie got me involved in a situation that nearly scared me to death, when somehow this shady character had Reggie's money. I don't know how the guy got it or why, only that he had it. Reggie was furious and wasn't about to stand for it.

"I'm going for my money," he said when he picked me up one night. I thought we were going to the movies.

"Man, you must be crazy," I told him. "You can't mess with that dude. He carries a gun."

"Maybe," Reggie said. He was totally calm. "But that son of a bitch is going to give me my money."

Reggie drove to a park where gangs used to hang out. He slowly circled it, checking out the people along the way. When he spotted his man, he pulled over to the curb and got out.

"Wait a minute," I said. "What am I supposed to do?"

"Whatever you want."

I followed Reggie a few feet and then ducked behind a tree. I didn't know what was going to happen. I was scared, super scared. I didn't want to have anything to do with guns. I couldn't believe Reggie. He walked right up to the dude, through all his people, and demanded the money. The dude handed it right over to him. After Reggie put the money in his pocket, we got out of there quickly. Little Reg was a fireball, the only person who could get me into something like that.

People from all over the city, whites as well as blacks, turned out for Reggie's funeral. His teammates, dressed in Everett High warm-ups, were pallbearers. I couldn't cry that day; I was all cried out. But others did. As a tribute to Reggie, we dedicated the next season to his memory.

The more my reputation grew, the more bothersome things became for several school officials, particularly the principal, Dr. Frank Throop. His office became the nerve center for dealing with ticket scalpers, college recruiters, and local businessmen requesting appearances. Dr. Throop appreciated the publicity for the school and said he didn't mind the extra work.

Requests for appearances became too numerous for me to handle or to even contemplate handling, but I always did what I could for the boys' clubs. I put on clinics, visited hospitals and schools, and simply hung out in the streets with the kids. I was the Pied Piper; kids followed me all day long. Sometimes I'd buy them ice cream cones and take them over to the playground to shoot around. It was fun for them as well as for me.

Entering my senior season I had total confidence in my game. I'd made first-team All-State as a junior and now was a preseason All-America selection. The game came so easily to me that I thoroughly dominated our first four or five games, scoring 30, 40, or whatever I decided that particular day. My teammates became more and more incidental with each game, a trend Fox worried about. Just before Christmas vacation, he summoned me to his office.

"Earvin," he said sternly, "I don't know if this is going to make any sense to you or not, but you're doing too much.

You're so dominating and so good, you intimidate your teammates. They wind up standing around and watching you just like everybody else in the building, including yours truly. They're reluctant to do anything for fear of making a mistake and making you mad.

"Our goal is to win the state championship. I know you want that more than anything in the world. So do I. But I don't know if we can do it the way we're playing now. Somewhere down the line we're going to need one of your teammates in a crucial stituation and he won't be ready to produce. I think if you cut down your scoring to twenty-something a game, we'll win it all."

"I hear you, coach," I said. Fox was right.

I immediately changed my game. I spread the points around, filled in where we were lacking, and took control offensively only when absolutely necessary. I weaved myself in and out of the flow of the game, acting as a kind of wild card. And as my scoring average dipped—down to 23 for the season—overall team effectiveness increased.

We steamrollered teams and didn't play a tight game until we went up against Jay Vincent and Eastern late in the regular season. We were No. 1 in the state, Eastern No. 2. The game was so big it was moved to Jenison Field House on the Michigan State campus. Eastern got out in front early and stayed there. It was our first defeat of the year. Then Eastern lost the next week.

As luck would have it, in the state tournament we drew Eastern in the district playoffs, the first round. A team goes from the districts to the regionals to the state quarterfinals to the semis to the finals. This time we played in Eastern's new gym and before the television cameras. A local station bought the rights to the game.

We beat them easily. Once out in front, we spread out on the court which gave me room to break my man down one-on-one. Defensively, we thoroughly frustrated Jay. Knowing he habitually put the ball on the floor before making his move, we collapsed on him at every opportunity and tried to strip the ball as soon as he dribbled. We were very successful at it and held him to one field goal and two free throws.

We rolled to the finals, where we met Brother Rice of Birmingham, Michigan, before a sellout crowd at Chrysler Arena on the campus of the University of Michigan. Brother Rice, a perennial basketball power, took us into overtime, but we beat them.

The championship. Finally.

It's too bad you can't be frozen into the precise moment of victory because it ends too quickly. After that championship, Coach Fox stayed at Everett two more years, knowing he had had his moment and probably wouldn't have another. He then resigned and took a job with the city in the placement center downtown.

"It made an old man out of me for the next three or four years," he once said. "You get used to success and winning, and when it is over, you wonder what kind of future you have. I knew chances were I'd never win like that again, so when the opportunity for one of those nice cushy jobs in education came up, where you don't have to lock yourself up in a classroom, I took it."

And I moved on to new coaches, including one—years later—who was the catalyst for the most controversial incident of my life.

4

Who Fired Coach Westhead?

EARLY SEASON—1981-82

November 19, 1981
It happened only yesterday, but it seems as if a week has already gone by. I was sitting on a stool, still sweating and still wearing my warm-ups, when the door to the visitors' locker room was opened to reporters. The first one, a Salt Lake City writer, looked around the room for a moment before settling on me.

"You guys should take it easy on the poor Jazz," he said with an ingratiating smile. Each reporter has his own way of opening a postgame interview. This was the lighthearted, chitchat approach.

"Take it easy on them?" I said in mock surprise. This was the required volley. "They should take it easy on us."

"What about Silk?" He had his pad out and his pen touching paper. It was time to go to work.

"What about him?" I smiled.

"Well, he's been in a terrible shooting slump, and tonight he snaps out of it and you win. How important is it that he shoot well?"

Jamaal, who had been shooting poorly through most of this early 1981–82 season, had had the jumper operating smoothly against the Jazz. He'd made 11 of 15 shots, scored 26 points, and was largely responsible for the 113–110 win, our fifth in a row and seventh in eleven games for the season. But we didn't look like a team on a roll. There wasn't any laughter. Nobody even smiled. We looked like a team that had just finished a night's work.

"When Silk's on as he was tonight," I explained, "he opens up the middle for the rest of us because the guy guarding him has to go out and get him. It especially makes Kareem's job easier. Silk's man is one less guy he has to deal with."

The Los Angeles writers arrived about then and formed a semicircle around me. One interrupted to ask, "What was that meeting between you and Westhead all about?" That was the jolt approach.

"One minute," I said. "Let me finish this up first."

I returned my attention to the Salt Lake City writer and continued. "We need Silk in the groove because it's too hard on the rest of us to make up for the twenty-some points he gets you night in and night out."

I turned back to the guys from L.A.

"I can't play here anymore," I said. "I want to leave. I want to be traded. I can't deal with it any longer. I'm going in to talk to the Man and ask him to trade me."

A crowd started to form. The writer from Salt Lake City, who'd started to back away, made a quick U-turn. You could almost hear the screech as he hit the brakes.

"Do you know what you're saying?" one reporter asked. I nodded.

"What happened in the meeting with Westhead?"

"Ask him."

"He won't say."

"If he ain't saying . . ." I wondered if I should get into it, then decided against it. "It was just something that happened, a little thing. He thought I wasn't listening to him. It was a minor thing."

"What brought this on?"

"I haven't been happy all season, and I'm not happy now. I've got to go."

"What are you unhappy about?"

"Things just haven't been—I don't know. I see certain things happening. I've tried to sit back, hoping they would pass, but they haven't. I haven't said anything before. Now I am. I've got to go. This is nothing against the guys. I love them. It's been a great experience playing with them, but now I've got to go. I feel all I'm doing is showing up and picking up a check. It's no fun. I can't play that way."

"Does Paul have anything to do with your unhappiness?"

"Some. We don't see eye to eye on certain things. It doesn't matter anymore. It's time for me to go. I'm going to talk to the Man. Hopefully, tomorrow. Definitely, tomorrow."

I stood up, grabbed my jacket out of the locker, and put it on over my warm-ups. Since the arena was located only a few blocks from the hotel, I had dressed in my room before the game and planned to shower there after.

"That's it, fellas," I told them as I reached for my cassette recorder and headphones. "You got your story. There isn't any more to say."

With that I put on my headphones, turned on some sounds, grabbed my equipment bag, and walked out of the locker room and towards the team bus. As one of the first on board, I took a seat in the back and tuned out by getting into my music. I stared blankly out the window, barely conscious of the fans jumping up and down to attract my attention below my window and of the players working their way through the crowd.

The news traveled quickly. After I left, the reporters interviewed Westhead and the rest of the players. Westhead expressed surprise. He said he was totally unaware of my unhappiness. The players were stunned, too, but more with the way it went down. Publicly, they had little to say; privately, most of them sympathized with me.

"You all right?" Nixon asked as he sat down across the aisle.

I nodded. I turned down the music on the cassette player.

Kareem took the seat in front of me and turned around.

"Do you want to talk about it, Earvin?" he asked.

"Not really," I said. I figured I'd already said enough for one night.

"Is it the offense?" he pressed.

"Part of it, Big Fella. It's only designed for you."

Kareem, having nothing further to add, turned to face the front.

Norm then leaned towards me and talked softly.

"Do you know what you got yourself into?"

"Yeah," I said, "I think so."

"I hope it's worth it."

"There was nothing else I could do. I've been talking to my father and Tuck almost every day for the last couple of weeks. We've been talking about it on the bus all the time. Nothing gets done. There's been too much talking and not enough doing. If this is how it's going to be, fine. I just don't want to be part of it."

"I don't want you to leave," Norm said.

"I don't want to leave. But I can't take it."

Coop arrived and stood in the aisle. The bus hadn't moved yet. We were waiting for Curran and a few more players. Westhead sat up front by himself. Our assistant coach, Pat Riley, apparently had gotten a ride to the hotel.

"You okay, Buck?" Coop asked.

"So far," I said. I smiled for him. Coop's a sensitive guy, and I could see he was upset.

"You can't leave," he said. "That wouldn't be right."

"Maybe not, but I gotta go."

We'd been sealed off from Westhead and had been stew-
ing over our problems. I didn't blame Kareem. He has a
natural aloofness that is as much his signature as the skyhook. He isn't the type of player you run around with at
home or on the road; you don't drop by his hotel room to
rap; and you certainly don't take your problems to him. He
closes out the kind of personal contact most players thrive
on. While many of us suffocated through the first three
weeks of the regular season, Kareem traveled his own road,
apparently oblivious to the team's general frustration. As a
result, we had nobody to turn to.

Westhead had coached with a unique self-effacing and
homespun approach his first season. This had ingratiated
him to players, reporters, and fans alike. Originally assistant
coach, he became interim head coach thirteen games into
the 1979–80 season, replacing his longtime friend Jack
McKinney, who had suffered serious head injuries in a freak
bicycle accident near his home. After we won the NBA
championship in 1980, Buss named Westhead head coach
outright and signed him to a four-year, $1.1-million con-
tract. Westhead retained McKinney's offensive system,
which worked, and frequently requested our input to solve
problems. But eleven games into this season, his third, he
was an embattled and lonely figure, a man consumed by a
need for total control. Following the first season he'd steadi-
ly removed himself from personal contact with the team.
Not only did he no longer seek our advice—he disdained it
when it was offered.

By the beginning of the season, he had completed the
installation of his own offense, a process he'd begun the
previous year. It highlighted Kareem's talents almost exclusively. Westhead was completely mesmerized by Kareem—
the man as well as the player. Because the skyhook is
undeniably the best percentage shot in the game, Westhead
figured it was the ideal shot to take in the set offense every
time.

Opponents easily defended it. By packing the middle, they made it difficult for us to make clean passes into Kareem and to cut through and set the picks required by the offense. We were immobilized. Everything, it seemed, got tipped or stolen. Instead of being a natural by-product of the offensive flow, getting a decent shot required a near-monumental effort. And if Norm or I dared break a play to create something on our own, Westhead called time-out to admonish us.

"You're not running the offense," he'd say. "You have to run it all the way through." Then, as we were going back on court, he'd add, "Okay, I want three passes this time, then into Kareem." These admonishments, though gentle in the beginning, grew harsher.

We were a team of high-priced talent. Kareem, Norm, Silk, Mitch, Coop, and I all made big salaries. And when you make that kind of money, you feel obligated to show you're worth it. But in Paul's system, we might as well have been journeymen carrying Kareem's sweats. It was a one-man show and a waste of the owner's money. "Run the offense" became the team slogan—and we'd run it, set the picks, and cut off them, but nothing ever happened.

While going to the bench for a time-out during one game, Norm said, "Coach . . ."

That's all he could get out of his mouth before Westhead jumped on him. "Goddamnit, Norman. How many times do I have to tell you? Run the damned offense and it'll work."

Norm was mad. "Man," he said to me as he sat down. "I wasn't even talking about the offense. I'm getting burned to death on picks out there and I'd like to know what the hell he wants done about it."

Westhead further demoralized us by calling all the plays from the bench. As soon as we'd take possession, he'd leap up and signal with his hands, usually the "fist up" play or the "five up," both of which were designed for Kareem. Westhead claimed he was a fast-break coach while at the same time he was curtailing our running game and molding

us into a slow-down, set-offense-type team. During the time
it takes for a coach to decide the play he wants, make the
signal, and have the player on court recognize the signal,
the fast break is dead. Besides, Norm and I were capable of
calling plays. We knew what was going on, who needed a
shot, who was hot, where the mismatch was, which play was
working.

After a while I gave up any hope of getting through to
Paul. Every time I tried to say something, I got the same
response: "You're not running the offense hard enough."
He clearly intended to continue forcing it on us. Something
was bound to happen.

That first occurred to me following the opening game of
the regular season. We played the Houston Rockets at the
Forum, which was appropriate in that we had closed the
previous season against the same team in the same building.
I was really excited. A new season, the Rockets. What a way
to begin, I thought. I wanted to run the Rockets off the
court, beat them badly as final proof that the problems of
the previous April had been resolved once and for all.

But the game turned into another nightmare. It was
another grind-it-out, low-scoring, slow-paced game that was
more to the Rockets' advantage than to ours. I hit a three-
point shot from about forty feet to put the game into
overtime, but we lost by a point in the second overtime.
The key play began when I grabbed a defensive rebound
with about fifteen seconds to go in the second overtime. We
led by a point, and all we had to do was waste the clock. As I
took the ball upcourt, I looked to the bench, having already
been conditioned to see what Westhead wanted done. He
was up hollering, only I couldn't hear him. I thought he had
a play, or possibly even wanted a time-out. Knowing he
wanted something but not knowing what, I picked up my
dribble in the backcourt and called time-out as the Houston
defenders closed on me.

As it turned out, he was excited and hollering for me to
kill the clock. The unnecessary time-out subsequently cost

us the game when Silk's inbounds pass to Kareem was long. It bounced off Kareem's hands and out of bounds, giving the ball to Houston with eleven seconds remaining. They had no trouble putting the ball inbounds and won the game on a basket by Moses Malone.

That was October 30. The Jazz game was less than three weeks later. The ship went down quickly. In our first road game, a defeat to the Trail Blazers in Portland, we walked the ball up the court almost the entire fourth period and, on orders from the bench, went into Kareem every play. He played a tremendous game and nearly pulled it out by himself.

We were very upset afterwards. The locker room in the Portland Coliseum is divided into two rooms. I shared one with Norm, Coop, Silk, Jim Brewer, and Eddie Jordan. As the last one in, I shut the door behind me.

"Man," I said as I sat down.

"Same old stuff," said Norm.

On the other side of the room, Silk was shaking his head. He's supposed to be our best perimeter shooter, but he didn't get a decent shot off the set offense all night.

"I can't believe it," I said. "What are we supposed to be doing out there?"

The room was so heavy with frustration I could barely lift my arms.

"Does anybody know?" I asked.

"I have no idea what our offensive concept is," said Silk. "I'm just going to go out and shoot and not worry about it."

"I've been telling you for two years," said Nixon, "the man cannot coach."

"Say something to the man, Nick," said Coop.

"It doesn't do any good. He won't listen, especially to me."

Curran opened the door and entered. He held up a couple of tape cutters. "Anybody need these?" he asked. He tossed one to Silk, another to Coop.

" Hey, thanks, Jack," Coop said with a big grin on his face.

"That's really nice of you to go out of your way and bring those in here."

We all cracked up. Jack frowned and started walking out. "Shut the door, Jack," I yelled, but he left it open. Eddie reached over to close it.

Soon, the door opened again. This time it was Westhead who entered. Everybody got quiet and began undressing. I stood up and faced my locker while stripping off my uniform. I glanced over to Norm, who was next to me, and suppressed a grin. Norm raised his eyebrows.

Westhead stood in the middle of the room for a moment. He then walked over to Norm and stiffly said, "Nice game, Norm." He turned around and walked out. Eddie reached out and closed the door again.

"Nick," said Coop, laughing. "The man's Main Man."

Everybody laughed.

"Nice game, my son," I said.

Norman cackled.

We all headed into the showers, where we continued laughing and ragging Norm over his new favorite-son status. The mood had lightened up considerably.

Several reporters entered the room just as we came out of the showers. We were still laughing, which, under the circumstances, struck them as strange. One writer asked me why I was laughing.

"I ain't saying nothing," I said. "You guys have been around long enough to see what's happening."

"Is it the offense?"

"Ask Norm," I said.

They went to Norm.

"No, not me," he said. "Go ask Coop."

We were smiling. Coop sent them to Silk, who while smiling coyly put his hands over his eyes, then his ears, then his mouth.

Later, Silk said, "I don't want to talk about the offense in the papers." Asked if he was worried, he added, "I'm not worried, but I'm beginning to get a little concerned."

The next night we got our first win of the season—by three points over the SuperSonics in Seattle. Then we lost again—by two points to Phoenix at the Forum. We were supposed to be one of the most explosive, fast-breaking teams in the league, yet we couldn't light a match, let alone light up the scoreboard.

Understand, the pressure to win in Los Angeles is enormous. Nothing less than a championship satisfies the fans and the media. And the players apply pressure on themselves as well. We know how much talent we have and how much money was spent in assembling it. We understand the expectations and accept the challenge.

Dr. Jerry Buss charges up to $22.50 ($75 for the VIP seats on court) for seats to Laker games and promises in return exciting, fast-breaking basketball, a style he calls "showtime." We weren't providing that kind of entertainment and Buss was displeased; I could tell by reading the expression on his face.

He enters the locker after every home game, accompanied by an entourage that includes his celebrity guests of the evening. Over the years, they have included a wide variety of show business and sports stars, including Sean Connery, Don Rickles, Reggie Jackson, Gabe Kaplan, Steve Martin, O. J. Simpson, Dom DeLuise. Usually he is all smiles, going from player to player and congratulating each on the victory if appropriate, or for playing a fine game, or whatever. After the Phoenix game, though he still made the round of players, he was noticeably tight-lipped and grim-faced. At my stall he asked me to stop by his office when I finished dressing.

To reach Dr. Buss's office I walked through the press lounge. It's always crowded after games—with members of the media and their friends, Forum employees and their friends, players' wives and their friends, and friends of friends and their friends. Sometimes I stop by the press lounge or Forum Club and talk for a while before leaving. But I wasn't in the mood for socializing. I quickly moved through there with my eyes focused straight ahead and my ears purposely closed. Rosemary Garmong, Buss's secretary, told me Buss was expecting me and to enter. I sat in the chair in front of his desk and, while he talked on the telephone, grabbed the jar of jelly beans he keeps in his office. He soon hung up and turned his attention to me. He wore his usual outfit—worn blue jeans, open-necked shirt, and boots. He leaned back in the chair and put a boot on the edge of the desk.

"What is wrong with this team, Magic?" he asked.

I expected the question. I smiled and shook my head. "I don't know. I really don't. We're just not in synch or something."

"Is it Paul?"

"I don't know if it's Paul or not. He works hard, I know that. I don't know. We just can't break loose. I know I feel uncomfortable."

"Is it the offense?"

"Part of it's the offense. We don't have it down yet."

"I just don't like the looks of the team. We look too much like we did in the playoffs last year. It seems like we're walking it upcourt too much."

"Yeah," I said. "We haven't been able to run the way we can."

"How're the guys doing?"

"Everybody's fine. You know, it's tough when you're losing, but we seem to be hanging in there pretty good. We have too much talent. We know it's only a matter of time before we bust one open."

"I hope so," he said.

The headline in the next day's sports section was the first public indication that Westhead was in trouble. It read: WESTHEAD GETS VOTE OF CONFIDENCE FROM BUSS.

I thought to myself, Wow, this is getting heavy. In pro

sports, an owner's vote of confidence is an indicator of bad news for the coach.

"I'm disappointed but not worried," Buss said in the newspaper story. "The way I see it is we're breaking in a new system and that takes time...."

When asked if Westhead's job was in jeopardy, Buss had replied, "No way. Paul has a four-year contract."

A day after that, Wilkes was quoted in a newspaper story as saying, "Something is just not right here in Lakerland.... It's a feeling, a rhythm, a timing that just isn't here. We had in the last two years and now we have to do some soul-searching to find out what happened to it. I, for one, don't understand...."

By this time Westhead was feeling the pressure mounting. He and Pat Riley modified the offense daily, but the changes were slight and superficial. They designed an option for Silk, hoping he would break out of his shooting slump. They added a play for Norm. But they never tampered with the foundation of the offense—the overreliance on Kareem.

We beat Dallas by only ten points. It shocked me that the Mavericks made a game of it.

Before the game I had lunch with two Dallas rookies, Mark Aguirre and Jay Vincent. Jay and I were still good friends. Mark, a three-time All-American at DePaul, is represented by my lawyers, George and Harold Andrews.

Jay and Mark didn't want to hear about my problems. They had enough of their own, mostly the big one of being on a losing team. When Dallas sportswriters found out about our lunch, they asked me what we had discussed. They were excited. I guess they suspected something deep had gone down.

"Sorry to disappoint you, fellas," I said, "but it was nothing. Just good friends taking advantage of an opportunity to get together. I told them to keep their chins up and things would get better."

"How would you deal with it if you were in Aguirre's situation?" one of the reporters asked.

"I'm not going to be on a loser," I said, "so I have to think we'd be winning more games."

"Why?"

"I don't know. . . . I've never been on a loser, ever."

"Does that mean you never will?"

"I'm just saying that I haven't. I'm never going to think like a loser or think I am one. I've been on pickup teams with guys who weren't very good and beaten five guys who were better. I don't know what it is, but before we even start, I tell my guys we can win if we do this, this, and this. And that's what happens."

But none of that was happening with the Lakers. I was playing with guys who were great and losing to guys who weren't.

We hit rock bottom two days later, November 10, in a game against the Spurs in San Antonio. We lost by twenty-six points, our worst defeat of the regular season, and failed to make a move on the Spurs the entire second half. What's more, the Spurs bombed us without George Gervin, their leading scorer and best player by far. San Antonio was a good team, but not that good.

Our offense was disgraceful. We wasted at least half the twenty-four-second clock just setting up. Then we had to scramble. If possible, we passed in to Kareem; if not, somebody forced a jump shot from the perimeter to beat the clock. Personally, I was humiliated. I had never been on a team that played so laxly.

Westhead jumped all over us in the locker room. "It was like they shoved their fists up your asses and twisted and you screamed for more and more" was his vivid summary of the game. I thought, Oh, man, let me get on that bus and get out of here before I scream.

Back at the hotel, I called Tuck and told him I was really unhappy. Ever since the Houston game, I had been in daily contact with Tuck and my father. They knew how I felt.

Whenever I'd get down—which was often—and suggest that playing somewhere else might be better for all concerned, they'd normally tell me to cool it. They'd say I'd feel better after a couple of wins. But this time they didn't try to appease me.

"Tuck," I said, "I've had it. I want to go in and ask Dr. Buss to trade me."

"Mmmmm," said Tuck. "That bad, huh?"

"Yeah, that bad."

"Look, I know Dr. Buss isn't happy, either. Why don't you sleep on it and we'll talk some more tomorrow."

Then I called my father.

"Man," I said. "I don't know what's going on."

"I understand how you feel," he said. "Whatever you feel you have to do, just do it. I brought you up to be open and honest about things, and to say and do what you think is right. Whatever you decide, I'm behind you."

I didn't sleep that night. I decided to meet with Buss in two days, as soon as we returned from the road trip. I felt this overriding uneasiness that I was flat out stealing his money. I was convinced that a trade was the only solution.

All night I rehearsed scenarios. I wanted to be firm, but at the same time I didn't want to come off as a spoiled brat. I wanted to be honest, but at the same time I didn't feel it was my place to indict Westhead.

The next day my head felt as though it had been trapped in a buzz saw. The team traveled from San Antonio to Houston for a game that night against the Rockets. Outside the airport, while waiting for luggage to be put in the bus, I wandered away from the group and sat on a concrete divider. I closed my eyes and turned up my face to a warm patch of sunlight. And my mind raced on. Yes, I want a trade. No, I don't. Yes, no, yes, no. Finally, and once again, yes, yes, yes!

I called Tuck as soon as I got to my hotel room. I told him I'd made up my mind: I wanted to be traded. After a lengthy discussion, he suggested I allow him to present the case to Buss. That was fine with me, I said. That afternoon I slept soundly.

We beat the Rockets but we played poorly. We scored only ninety-five points.

Tuck talked to Buss the following day, Thursday, November 12. Tuck said I was displeased with the way the team was playing. He decided against telling Buss I wanted to be traded.

"You've got to suck it in for now," Tuck told me following his conversation with Buss. "Make sure you're doing your job the best you can do. I know your stats are good, but stats aren't everything. And watch your overall attitude."

"My attitude's fine," I snapped. "I'm doing everything I can."

"Okay, good. Just concentrate on playing ball. Dr. Buss is aware that problems exist and will do something to correct them if they continue. I don't think this is a good time for you to go in there."

So I didn't.

Beginning the next night, we played three games in as many nights: first Portland at home, then Phoenix on the road, and then Indiana at home Sunday night. Although we won all three, nobody regarded the wins as a breakthrough. Against Phoenix, we scored only fourteen points in the fourth period and barely managed to hold off the Suns by one. Against Indiana we blew an eight-point lead with two minutes to go and won by a point in double overtime.

Westhead and Riley became obsessed with the situation to the point where they believed the players, or a few of them anyway, were undermining their efforts. Norman, who believed in speaking his piece, usually came under suspicion.

During a time-out against Phoenix, Norm came back to the bench saying, "We've got to get more move—"

This time it was Riley who pounced on him before he could complete the thought. "The offense works!" Riley screamed. "You guys just ain't running through it."

"Damn," I said under my breath. Norm just sighed.

I would think a coach would welcome a player's input. The players know what's happening. They have a feel for the game that a coach cannot possibly have. They feel the picks, they feel the muscle being thrown around under the boards, they feel the hot hand; only a player can look into the eyes of a defensive man and see if fear exists or not. Coaches tap all sorts of sources for information: scouting reports, videotapes, magazines, newspapers, stat sheets, NBA gossip. Yet some ignore the firsthand knowledge at their fingertips.

Unknown to me and the other players, Buss had decided to fire Westhead. The decision had been made in a meeting with the general manager, Bill Sharman, and special consultant Jerry West at 4:30 on the afternoon of the Indiana game. The decision was unanimous, according to Buss. But it was not carried out immediately because West, Buss's choice to succeed Westhead, refused the job. They decided to wait a week, until Monday, November 23, during which time Buss hoped to change West's mind, or twist his arm, if necessary, while Sharman also investigated the availability of a coach currently working as an assistant in the NBA.

I learned that during that meeting before the Indiana game, Buss made a prophetic statement. "What happens," he said, "if something blows up during the week? Maybe we should go ahead and fire the coach today." Sharman and West assured him a blowup was unlikely. Nonetheless, it occurred three days later. That was when I told the reporters in Utah that I wanted to be traded.

Westhead has since claimed he had no knowledge of the meeting held the afternoon of the Indiana game. He's said he did not even feel his job was in jeopardy. But he was noticeably quiet and tense the day before the Utah game. On the flight to Salt Lake City he even jumped on our trainer, Jack Curran.

Before road trips, each member of the Laker traveling party receives an itinerary. It specifies such standard information as flight departures and arrivals, carriers and flight numbers, hotels, game times, and practice times. Also noted is the in-flight meal: breakfast, lunch, dinner, or snack. According to the itinerary, dinner was supposed to be served on the flight. When a snack arrived instead, Westhead reread the itinerary and griped to Jack.

"It says here dinner," he said. "If I knew we were only getting a snack, I would've eaten at home."

Jack apologized, trying to explain that a simple mistake had been made. Paul growled and then ate the sandwich. He was sitting alone, which was unusual. In the past he and Riley had always sat together. But by this time, events had strained even their relationship, which once was almost brotherly.

Westhead made additional changes in the offense during shoot-around the next morning. He was grim and serious, all business. Then in the game—another close one—he was jumping off the bench calling all the plays, leaving nothing to chance, nothing to us. After Mark Landsberger forced a long jumper that missed by a mile, Westhead called time-out exclusively to berate him.

"That's not your shot!" he screamed. "That's not your shot. I keep telling you to run the offense." And on and on. I stood back and looked at the man. His face was flushed and twisted, the bloodshot eyes bulged. Watching a coach fall, I thought, wasn't pretty.

Late in the game he turned on me twice. Now, I hadn't complained to him about anything in weeks. Whatever he asked me to do, I did. I worked hard in practice, and I tried to make the offense work. My attitude had never been questioned in my life, nor had I ever been accused of being inattentive to a coach. My mind is focused on the game from the opening tip to the final buzzer. The game is my life.

Against Utah, while walking to the huddle for a time-out, I talked to Mitch Kupchak. Darryl Griffith had just burned me twice because Mitch had inadvertently picked me, and

I wanted to get it straightened out. As we reached the bench and sat down, we kept talking.

"Just keep an eye out," I said, "and open up more on your. . ."

"Shut up, E. J.," interrupted Westhead. He was nervous and anxious. "I got it. I got it. Be quiet. I got it. . . ."

I didn't say anything, but I steamed.

Utah called time-out a few minutes later. Silk had just made two free throws to give us a four-point lead with six seconds to go in the game. We all let out a big sigh of relief as we came to the bench. It was a struggle, but we felt we'd made it through.

As I took the first seat on the bench and began mopping the sweat from my face, I heard some guy hassling me from the stands immediately behind the bench. Instinctively, I turned around.

"You too, Magic," snapped Westhead. "Turn around, E. Pay attention when I'm talking."

"I *am* listening," I answered. I really fumed. As soon as the buzzer sounded, signifying the end of the time-out, I got up and walked on court, where I stood by myself for several seconds. Westhead didn't even notice; Riley pointed it out to him.

I went straight to the locker room after the game. I was mad, but I wasn't going to say anything, even though I thought about it. As always, win or lose, we huddled up in the locker room, putting our hands together in a show of unity, and said, " 'Ray, team."

Westhead intercepted me on my way to my locker. "Magic," he said, motioning me outside. I followed him ten feet down the corridor to a small, nine-foot-by-twelve-foot dressing room. The room, painted stark white, had a vanity mirror along one wall and a small bathroom and closet in the back. Westhead closed the door and stood with his back to it.

"Don't you ever do that to me again!" he raged. I thought to myself, That's it, I don't have to deal with this.

And he went on: "Don't you dare talk back to me and say, 'I'm listening.' Just keep your mouth shut and pay attention to me. I could've showed you up in front of the others, too."

"Is that all?" I asked. I reached for the doorknob, but he pressed his back to the door.

"No, that's not all," he said. "I'm tired of your crap. You don't walk out of the huddle like that on me. I'm sick and tired of your horseshit attitude."

I kept calm on the outside. Inside, I boiled. Finally, he jerked the door open. I walked through the reporters congregated outside the locker room. I knew then I'd had it.

"That's it, guys," I said to the team in general as I entered the locker room and headed towards my locker. "It's been great. I had a lot of fun and I love you all, but I'm out of here. I'm going to play somewhere else."

Nixon looked over. "Easy, Buck," he said.

"No, that's it," I continued. "I'm through. I don't have to take this anymore. I'm going in tomorrow to ask the Man to trade me."

Then the reporters came in.

I spent much of the night on the telephone, talking mostly with my father and Tuck. My father was very supportive. He knew something had to give. When I explained what had happened during the time-outs and in the meeting with Westhead after the game, he understood why I was the one who set off the explosion.

"As long as you feel deep in your heart that what you did was right, then you have nothing to fear or be ashamed of," he said. "Just hold your head high and take what happens with dignity."

He asked me how the other players reacted. I told him they were shocked but that most supported me.

"Who supports you?" he asked.

"Norm and Coop, Jim Brewer, Mark Landsberger, Eddie

Jordan. Silk I know is unhappy. And Mitch is so confused he
has no idea what's going on."

"What about Kareem?"

"I don't know. He's in his own world, so I don't think he
cares one way or the other."

"Did anybody support you publicly?"

"No, not yet."

"Will they?"

"I don't know. Maybe eventually."

Tuck, meanwhile, wanted to know all the details, every
word that was spoken and every gesture made.

"Were you listening to him in the huddle?" he asked.

"Yes, I told you I was listening." I was getting exasperated.

"Okay, just want to make sure."

He called back later. It was in the middle of the night. He
said he had talked to a few people at the Forum who said
Buss had already arranged a meeting with Sharman and
West in the morning.

"What should I do tomorrow?" I asked.

"Just go home," he said. "And I don't think you should say
anything further to the press until this thing is resolved."

"They'll be out at the airport," I said.

"Just say 'No comment,' that's all."

Buss was watching a Los Angeles Kings–Detroit Red
Wings ice hockey game at the Forum when he learned the
news. He has a telephone in his private box. Chick Hearn,
the Lakers' play-by-play announcer, made the call.

"Catastrophe," said Chick.

"What do you mean, Chick?" Buss asked. "What happened?"

"Magic announced he wants to be traded." Chick then
filled him in.

Buss's initial response was "Oh, crap."

Having been alerted by their newspapers, the reporters
covering the Kings' game converged on Buss's box for his

reaction. Buss said he was unaware of all the details and would discuss the matter with everyone concerned the following morning.

A horde of reporters, TV broadcasters, and cameramen met the team at the Los Angeles airport in the morning. I just walked on through, as politely as possible telling everybody who requested an interview that I had no further comment. I went home and got some sleep.

Buss met with Sharman and West. Buss suggested that in light of new events firing Westhead now might be terrible timing. Sharman and West, according to Buss, said it was a risk they had to take. Buss agreed, and appointed West as head coach. West still didn't want the job and began to lobby for Riley, saying he believed Riley could handle it. Buss then amended his position. He gave West full responsibility for coaching the Lakers, including the power to delegate as much or as little authority to Riley as he saw fit. The only stipulation Buss attached was an order that West get the offense moving again. West said he'd take care of that.

Their paths didn't cross again until the press conference several hours later. Which explains why it turned into such a farce. While Buss broke the news to Westhead, Sharman and West met with Riley. West appointed Riley head coach on an interim basis and appointed himself the temporary assistant.

Buss telephoned me after his meeting with Westhead. The ring jolted me from a deep sleep. For a moment I didn't know where I was or to whom I was talking. I came to when he told me what had happened.

"Magic," he said, "I want you to stay. Jerry West, Bill Sharman, and I decided to fire Paul last Sunday and were waiting to find a replacement. You shouldn't have said anything. You stuck your nose into the wrong place."

I tried to resume my nap, but couldn't. Later, I went to a swank Beverly Hills party. Buss was there, too. And Norm Nixon. Several people congratulated me for being brave enough to speak my mind. I was glad to hear some positive comments, because there'd already been a groundswell of indignation and anger.

Buss told me and Norm that they'd had a press conference to announce the new coach and that it had been a mess. He blamed himself. He said he should have checked with West, Sharman, or Riley before walking out to the dais and announcing West as the new offensive coach and Riley as the defensive coach. Because right after he'd done that, West had taken the microphone and said that Riley was the head coach—period.

Buss told us that he first considered replacing Westhead right after the loss to Houston in the season opener. "That Houston loss hurt," he said. "I had been waiting four months to kick Houston's ass. I wanted to ram it down their throats. I felt my players had to be so ticked off with what they had done to us—I know I was—that we'd win by forty points. When we lost, I went back into my old shock. What really confused me was the way we lost. It was the same struggle. If you watched the videotape and disregarded the cast of characters, which was slightly different, you'd sense a game flow similar to that in last season's playoffs.

"I'm watching this game over and over and finally I'm saying, 'Wait a minute. Here I've got great talent. He's had four months to work on it and I've given him a great new player in Kupchak, and he still gives me the same result. There's something wrong.'

"And there was. But I didn't say anything. After six games, when we were two-four, Sharman and West began saying, 'I don't like the way things are going. Something is wrong.' I knew then I had to make a move. Paul was forcing the talent to fit into a system, instead of building a suitable system to fit the talent. Even I could see that."

I listened quietly. There wasn't much to say. I felt bad that Westhead had lost his job, but I was relieved to learn I hadn't caused it. I would not have accepted that.

But I do know this: lots of fans and reporters aren't going to believe it. I'm excited that we may finally get a chance to break loose. But I also think I may be in for a pretty rough time.

Too bad, but I've been under pressure before.

5

The Recruiters

Back in my sophomore year in high school, a couple of days after we'd been beaten in the state quarterfinals, Coach Fox called me into his office. He smiled as he reached into his desk drawer and pulled out a manila envelope.

"Here," he said, handing it over.

"What is it?" I asked. His smile puzzled me.

"Open it up."

I opened the envelope and drew out four or five letters. Each one had a name of a university or college in the upper left-hand corner.

"Oh, man," I said in anticipation.

"Oh, man," I repeated as I started reading.

"Oh, man," I said as I read the second letter and then the third. "I can't believe this is happening." I read on.

I was fifteen years old, and for the first time I realized

that in all likelihood basketball was going to get me a college scholarship.

In each letter, the basketball coach congratulated me on a fine season. He wished me luck in the future, promised to follow my progress, and looked forward to a meeting at the appropriate time. He hoped I would consider his school when deciding where to continue my education.

"Oh, wow!" I screamed.

"Easy, Earv," said Fox. "This is only the beginning. What do you plan doing about those letters?"

"I don't know. Take them home."

"Well," he started, "don't you think you should answer them?"

"I guess so."

"I'll talk to Dr. Throop. Maybe he can have one of the school secretaries write up a reply saying how much you appreciate their interest in you, stuff like that. And you can sign it."

That was fine with me. Over the next two years, Everett High received more mail addressed to me than to everybody else in school combined. Somewhere along the line I lost track, but as far as I could tell, every school in the country that played basketball contacted me. Once the novelty wore off, I stopped reading the letters. There were so many; besides, they all said the same thing. Dr. Throop would ask me if I was interested in such-and-such school and then convey the appropriate reply.

Of course, a negative response did not stop the more aggressive recruiters. They telephoned my house at all hours of the day and night, showed up on my doorstep, and camped out at school. Saying no has always been difficult for me, but it was especially hard then. So I ended up with no time for myself.

This led to a few embarrassments. Like the times a recruiter who had scheduled a meeting with me would arrive at my house to find out he had been stood up. My mother covered for me as well as she could. She knew I was hiding out because I had agreed to an appointment I had no intention of keeping. This bothered her. But not as much as the telephone calls in the middle of the night.

"Is Earvin home?" asked one caller at two o'clock one morning.

"He's sleeping," she answered.

"I'm sorry to trouble you, but this is very important. Would you mind waking him?"

"I certainly would," she said indignantly. "He has school tomorrow."

"Then what time does he get up?"

As my mother remembers it, the majority of people who called were very pleasant and polite. But there were always a few who weren't. She says that the ten months prior to my signing a letter of intent for college were a harrowing time. Wooing the mother is one of the basic strategies of recruiting: if you can get to the mother, the theory goes, you can get to the son.

Some recruiters tried to make personal contact at school. One guy—from Maryland—must have been under instructions to stay in Lansing until he signed me. He befriended one of the administrative assistants and practically moved in. Dr. Throop was forced to bar him from the grounds during school hours.

Recruiters who offered cash and cars under the table were rejected immediately. They'd say, "What do you want?" I'd shrug and answer, "Nothing." Some were shocked. Before my junior year, Dr. Throop gave me a handbook outlining NCAA guidelines on recruiting. I studied it with Tuck, on whom I began to rely more and more for advice. In turn, he made sure my father always knew who was talking to me and what about. My father kept a low profile, and because of his long work hours, he was hassled less than anybody else by the recruiters.

We decided early on not to get involved with any under-the-table stuff. "If you're good enough," Tuck always said, "you'll get what's coming to you. Why mess with your future for a few things now?" Even though we were allowed to have meals purchased for us by the schools, we wouldn't accept them. If he was there, as he usually was, Tuck would pick up the entire tab himself or pay our share when it came time to pay the bill.

I didn't even make all the trips the NCAA allows. I visited only the campuses of Michigan, Notre Dame, Maryland, and North Carolina. Since Michigan State was down the road, I didn't have to make a formal visit there.

I could have made two more trips, and I was definitely interested in checking out UCLA. When you talked about college basketball in those days, you talked about UCLA— Coach John Wooden, Kareem, Bill Walton, ten NCAA championships. And when an assistant coach at the school, Lee Hunt, set up a date for me to visit, I looked forward to it for months.

But a week before I was supposed to go, Hunt called with bad news. He said there had been a mix-up, and asked if I'd mind postponing my trip and taking a weekend later in the school year so that they could accommodate Albert King and another player.

"It's now or never," I told him.

"Well, we can't do it now," he said.

I was kind of insulted. I figured they would have worked something out if they wanted me badly enough. So I struck UCLA from the list I kept and narrowed it down to five schools: North Carolina, Maryland, Notre Dame, Michigan, and Michigan State. Once the list made the rounds, the rush from recruiters representing the five schools intensified.

Through my entire senior year, trying to decide which college to attend was a constant tug-of-war. I talked to my father about it, to my mother, to Tuck, to my brothers and sisters, and to dozens more who were only too happy to offer their suggestions and opinions. But *I* had to make the decision, and it wasn't easy.

My father lobbied for Michigan State because it was close to home, but he always stopped short of telling me to go there. "Is that where you want me to go?" I asked him, I don't know, hundreds of times. Each time he gave the same answer: "It's up to you. You're old enough to make up your own mind."

One night early in my senior year a recruiter called the house and woke me up. I just happened to pick up the telephone. It was one of those mistakes. He talked for about an hour about the basketball program, the distinguished coach, the school's honorable athletic tradition, the beautiful new dormitories, the large, multifaceted on-campus arena, and on and on. Half-listening, I repeatedly said, "Uh-huh. Uh-huh." Then he started going on about the academic program and the significant advancements the school had made in biochemical and nuclear research. I thought, Be real. I recognized the importance of education, but we were talking basketball. He cared about as much for my education as he did for the ghetto children starving in his hometown.

In the beginning, I loved the idea of being recruited. It felt good to be wanted, to be fawned over. But it got old quickly. I got tired of the phony smiles, the insincere speeches, and the leers that accompanied the illegal offers. All I wanted to do was play basketball in college and then go into the pros.

I couldn't fall back to sleep after hanging up on the recruiter, so I drove to the garage where my father was working. Even though it was cool out, he was sweating heavily from lifting one-hundred-pound barrels onto his truck. I gave him a hand with a few of them.

"Easy," he said. "Be careful. You have to know how to lift these things."

After we finished loading the truck, we took a break. My father sat on a stoop; I sat beside him on the concrete. A bare bulb lighted the garage, which smelled of grease and gasoline.

"What's the matter?" he asked.

I told him about the recruiter's call and how much I disliked being in the middle of such a seamy business. He understood. But, as he said, it wasn't going to stop until I made up my mind. I asked him what he thought.

"You can go anyplace in the country," he said. "You have the opportunity of a lifetime. But you have to remember that if you go someplace that's quite a ways from here and something goes wrong, it may get out of hand before we know about it back home. If you go to Michigan State, on the other hand, and something happens, say they mistreat you, we'll know about it like that." He snapped his fingers for emphasis.

"And another thing you better remember. If you go to a place like UCLA, they're going to have a California boy as good or nearly as good as you, and he, quite naturally, will get a chance to play first. That's all I'm going to say about it. You decide. I'll be behind you."

I'd strongly favored Michigan State until my senior year. I grew up in its shadow, played ball there, followed and rooted for its teams, and liked and respected Gus Ganakas, its head basketball coach. But, to my surprise, Ganakas had been let go after my junior year at Everett and replaced by Jud Heathcote, a fire-and-brimstone coach. I didn't particularly like the idea of playing for a coach who hollered all the time.

My other main leaning was towards the University of Michigan, an easy drive about fifty miles up the road, in Ann Arbor. Besides having a better basketball tradition and more prestige overall, its location away from home, even though it was not that far away, attracted me. It was close enough, I figured, that I could get help if I needed it.

Like my father, Tuck tried to stay neutral. But, also like my father, Tuck nonetheless lobbied strongly for Michigan State. Mainly, he asked that I not prejudge Heathcote: "See what Heathcote's like, then decide."

My mother was the only one who favored the University of Michigan. Although basketball was my life, she was more concerned with the quality of education and believed Michigan's to be better. She considered education the key to success. And the better the education, the more doors it unlocked. She takes great pride in the fact that all her children have had at least some college experience.

Towards the end of my senior year, I formally eliminated Notre Dame and North Carolina. Two weeks later I scratched Maryland. Michigan and Michigan State were left. When it came right down to it, they were the only schools that I had ever seriously considered.

I didn't know what to do. I really liked Michigan—its people, its program, its campus, and its social life. I knew I not only would enjoy living there but, with its nucleus of good talent, I also believed I could be part of an NCAA championship team. On the other side was Michigan State, my hometown school—the preference of my father, Tuck, and my fans, which included a lot of kids who belonged to the boys' clubs I helped support. The kids begged me to go to Michigan State. I'd be trying to put on a clinic at one of the playgrounds around town, and they wouldn't even let me demonstrate. All they wanted to talk about was where I was going to go to school.

"Oh, Magic," they'd say, "you can't leave us and go to Michigan. You have to stay right here and be a Spartan." I'd laugh and tell them I'd have to think about it.

Shortly after we won the state championship, I was among a group of high school seniors selected to play in the Albert Schweitzer Games in West Germany. The timing was perfect. It let me get away from Lansing and take a look at my situation from another perspective.

We had a great time touring the U.S. military bases. The Americans there loved us and the way we tore up the competition. We played against teams from Italy, Russia, West Germany, Sweden, Yugoslavia, Spain, France, and

Holland. The players were supposed to be high school kids, but they weren't. Some were in their early twenties. It didn't really matter to us—nobody gave us any trouble. We played each team twice, and one team we beat by more than a hundred points each time. We typically won a game by 50 or 60.

Besides myself, we had five players who went on to play in the NBA: Eddie Johnson, Darnell Valentine, Tracy Jackson, Jeff Ruland, and Jeff Lamp. We also had Tommy Baker, a guard, who was Mr. Basketball in Indiana that year. He eventually beat me out as the tour's Most Valuable Player.

We drew light crowds the first two games. Then word got out, and we packed the gyms all over the country. We pressed and ran the other teams to death. The Americans in the stands went crazy, giving us standing ovation after standing ovation every game. I think we showed the Europeans a new way to play basketball. They reciprocated by taking us out on the town at every stop, to nice restaurants (where I ate German food for the first time), to discos, and to small private jazz clubs.

In every city, we'd be taken into town by bus at least one afternoon and allowed to wander around on our own. We were like creatures from outer space to the Germans, not because we were black but because we were so tall and black. They were very nice. They'd talk German to us and we'd try to respond. We'd all wind up laughing our heads off—the Germans, too.

In Mannheim, my favorite city on the tour, one middle-aged German woman who spoke passable English approached me and asked my name.

"Magic," I answered.

"Magic," she said. "Magic . . ." She kept repeating it. She didn't understand. "That ist no name," she said. She pronounced the words very slowly and carefully. "Vat ist your name?"

I guess she thought I couldn't understand her English; the

guys with me were cracking up. I smiled and answered very politely. "My name ist Magic Johnson," I said.

She smiled. "Really?" she said.

I nodded.

"That ist an unusual name."

"I am an unusual person," I told her.

She smiled again. "That I can see," she said.

On tour, I gave a lot of serious thought to choosing my college. Often I hung around the day room on the Army base, shooting pool with the team or playing Ping-Pong. We talked about our scholarship offers and where we were going. I kept saying, "I don't know. Michigan or Michigan State." But deep down, I started leaning back toward Michigan State.

When I came home, booster groups from both schools greeted me at the Lansing airport—Michigan on the left, Michigan State on the right. Each side held a banner that read WELCOME HOME, MAGIC. I felt like I was running for office. I walked straight ahead and located Tuck.

"What's going on?" I asked.

"It's almost time," he said.

I nodded. Grimly.

Two nights later I drove out to where my father was working. I knew Tuck would be there helping out.

"What do you think?" I asked.

"If you go to Michigan State, fine," my father said. "If you go to Michigan, fine. We'll watch you play wherever you go. But if you go to Michigan, we may not be able to see every game."

"What about you, Tuck?"

"I'll support you if you want to go to Michigan," he said. "I'll drive there every day if I have to. But don't go there because you think they have a better basketball program. I don't want to hear that. I don't want to hear about Michigan having Phil Hubbard and Alan Hardy and those people.

"It's true you might win up there. But there's talent right

here at Michigan State. You can win it here, too. If you
think you're that good, then you make the program. Don't
worry about going to a school that already has one."

The deadline for signing the letter of intent was in two
days, so I asked Tuck to arrange some kind of press conference with the people at Everett. I left and went home. The
next morning I talked to my mother.

"I made up my mind," I told her.

"Which one?" she asked. She smiled sweetly, as she always did.

"Michigan State."

Her smile dropped on me like a ton of bricks. "Are you
serious?" she asked in amazement.

"Yes."

"But I thought you wanted to go to Michigan?"

"I thought so, too," I said. "I liked the idea of going there
because they're on top, but I've always been for the underdog. I think I'll go through the underdog thing again and
see what happens."

Scholastically, I was in fine shape. My 2.8 grade-point
average was acceptable to Michigan and Michigan State, as
well as to any other school in the country, when taken in
conjunction with my scoring average. Both schools offered
the unsolicited guarantee that I would start as a freshman.
The scholarship offers were identical, with the standard
grant-in-aid: books, tuition, and room and board. There
were no strings attached, no "extras."

I called my father at work and asked him to meet me at
Tuck's house. There I told them it was Michigan State.

"You all happy now?" I asked.

I knew they were. But they protested, telling me not to
go there on their behalf, that it was up to me.

"There's no need to discuss anything more," I told them.
"It's done."

But there was much more to do. My father and I went to
Everett to inform Dr. Throop, who already had begun

organizing the press conference. It was to be held the following morning in the school auditorium. Dr. Throop, also pleased I had chosen Michigan State, immediately got on the telephone and dialed Heathcote.

"Jud," he said, smiling. "You interested in stopping by my office this afternoon? I think you should. It's about something important."

After hanging up, Dr. Throop turned to us and said, "He said he'll be here in five minutes."

Heathcote and Vern Payne, Heathcote's assistant, walked through the door precisely five minutes later. Payne was the Michigan State recruiter who'd worked the hardest to land me. His primary function, it turned out, was to sell me on Heathcote—a coach he liked and respected.

As might be expected, they were delighted to hear my decision. The year before—Heathcote's first year recruiting for Michigan State—they'd failed to sign any of the fourteen high school players they sought. This time, within a matter of weeks, they had landed Jay Vincent and me. My commitment would become official as soon as I signed the letter of intent—which suddenly appeared. As if by magic.

The following morning, members of the media from as far away as Chicago, New York, Florida, and Washington, D.C., jammed the two-hundred-seat Everett High School auditorium. All of the Detroit television stations and its two major newspapers were also well represented. It was the biggest thing to hit the auditorium since the senior play.

I walked onto the stage and took a seat at the head table. Word had not leaked out. But people representing the University of Michigan must have been uneasy that they had not been alerted.

At the head table I joined my mother and father, Tuck, Dr. Throop, and George Fox. A few students squeezed into the auditorium, but most stayed in their classrooms, where they listened to the proceedings over the public address system.

As I waited to begin, I felt a great inner calm. I totally blocked out the noise and confusion. I had made my decision, and I knew it was right.

"Earv," I heard Dr. Throop say, "you're on."

I nodded and walked to the microphones.

"I guess you all wondered why I called you here today," I said in a weak attempt at humor. It brought on polite laughter. "As many of you know," I continued, "I just returned from a two-week tour of Germany. It was the first time in my life that I had an opportunity to get away from home for that length of time, and I loved it. I had a great time. But while away, I came to realize how much I love Lansing and the people who live here and how impossible it is for me to leave. So I've decided to stay and attend Michigan State."

There was immediate activity. Reporters scrambled to reach the bank of telephones installed outside the auditorium. Then came the questions.

"Why Michigan State, Earvin?"

"I grew up here and always dreamed that someday I would wear the green and white. When it came right down to it, I don't think I could have gone anywhere else. I was born to be a Spartan."

"Do you feel you let Michigan down?"

"Yes, and I don't feel good about it. They were super to me and gave me a lot of their time, which I appreciate. I made friends and I hope they remain friends, which I'm sure they will. Either way, I had to let somebody down. I knew that all along. I was in a no-win situation."

"How do you feel about going to a school that doesn't have much of a basketball reputation?"

"I don't care about reputations, or what happened in the past. All I care about is the future, and I see an NCAA championship in Michigan State's."

6

Playing the College Game

I was an instant hit at Michigan State. The school had recently been under NCAA sanctions in football. There had been player dissension and suspensions in basketball under Ganakas. I guess I represented a fresh start.

On campus, I literally stopped traffic.

"Is that Magic?" I'd hear while heading for class.

"Yeah, must be."

"That's not his real name, is it?"

"I think so."

"Great name."

On and on it went. People from all walks of campus life— radical students, conservative students, foreign exchange students, men, women, professors, administrators, jocks, maintenance workers, and campus police—all stopped me to introduce themselves and to thank me for choosing Michigan State.

I moved into Wilson Hall, an on-campus dormitory. I roomed with Jay Vincent, took a full class load, and chose telecommunications as my major. From Day One I cracked the books. I studied hard and got a B average for the first quarter. Not bad for a jock, I thought.

I wanted to experience the entire educational experience, including campus nightlife. So I became a part-time disc jockey at a disco, Bonnie & Clyde's. E. J. the DeeJay.

Those first few weeks were the greatest. Not once did I regret my choice. In going to Michigan State, I enjoyed the best of both worlds—the freedom of living in the dorm and the comfort of being only a few miles from home. Occasionally I'd stop by the house for a meal and maybe to drop off a load of wash. My mother would ask me about my progress in school, then my father would take me aside to get the details about the afternoon workouts.

"I'm turning it out," I told him once.

"Be careful about coming on too strong," he warned. "Make sure you take care of the other guys."

"It's under control."

I always had it under control. I understood that glory could blow out just as easily as it blew in. The bottom line is always production.

Michigan State had last won the Big Ten championship in 1959. Since then it had been mostly a conference also-ran, the poor relation to Michigan. The team had been 10–17 in Jud Heathcote's first season. Now, in his second, with returning starters Greg Kelser and Bob Chapman, plus Jay Vincent and me, it figured to be better.

Jud is a funny man. Off court, he's the kind of guy who takes over airplanes, buses, hotel lobbies, everything. Really comical. But on court, he's a fiery coach who hates to lose. If it wasn't for that other side of his personality, I don't know if I could have accepted all his hollering, because I don't believe it is a necessary motivational tool. But Jud never loses control, even though at times he appears to. He's smart. He knows the game and can prepare a team as well as any coach I've ever seen. If he has the talent and the time to prepare, he'll win. You can count on it. He'll devise a defense that will smother the other team. That's his genius.

I couldn't sleep the night before my first game. I tossed and turned, my mind flashing with heroic deeds: throwing a perfect full-court behind-the-back pass, flying to the hoop for a jarring dunk, skying over everybody for the rebound. I could sense victory. I could hear the roar of the crowd. I could also feel my nerves.

By game time the butterflies in my gut were as large as hawks. My heart pounded. My mind raced. Since April, when I chose Michigan State, Jenison Field House had been sold out for this opener against Central Michigan. Every game I'd play at Jenison would be a sellout. Eventually, the athletic office devised a lottery system to distribute the 5,000 tickets available to the students.

The old building shook when the public address announcer introduced me and the rest of the starters. It continued to shake through the opening minutes and didn't subside until Central Michigan clearly took control of the game for a while. My teammates were tense, too. Fortunately they recovered, especially Jay, who scored 25 points. Although I never fully relaxed, I thought I did all right. I had 7 points, 9 rebounds and 8 assists. But I knew the fans, not to mention the reporters, left the building disappointed. I was just happy we won. There would be plenty of games down the line to make a better impression.

Kenny Turner, my good friend and most dedicated fan, was more disappointed than most. He had built me up sky-high before the game, telling people how the Big Ten had never seen a player like me, a big man who could run, score, handle the ball, and pass. I'd first met Kenny after a high school game. He'd introduced himself and asked if I would be interested in seeing the film he'd shot of the game. He said he was a movie-camera buff. I looked him over. He carried a Super Eight over one shoulder. I said sure. Once I did, it was all over. I wanted to see all the films he had of me. And he had plenty.

Kenny was a newspaper boy when he first became interested in my career. While on his route one day, he had stopped by Main Street to watch a few games because he had heard about a talented junior high school kid who played there. I was the kid, of course, and I guess I impressed him.

In the beginning I watched his films for the fun of it. I loved seeing myself on the screen and went wild over the good plays. But once the novelty wore off, I used the films as a teaching tool. I detected and corrected flaws in my game, made good moves better, and scouted players and teams for future games. I still use the tool, only now it's videotape.

Even before we became tight, Kenny would go around boasting about my game. After my Michigan State opener, I knew he'd be unhappy. And when I met him later that night, after dinner with my family, his unhappiness glowed in the dark.

"What did you think?" I asked.

"I don't know," he responded. He shrugged and adjusted his glasses.

"Hey, dude. Tell me."

"I didn't think much, to tell you the truth. I kept waiting for you to do something. Waiting and waiting and waiting."

"Me, too." I sighed and smiled. "I'm just glad it's over. Now I can get down and play some ball."

"The press is going to tear you up. They'll be writing: Magic? What Magic?" Kenny started looking around the room. "Where's the Magic? You see it?"

We laughed.

"That's all right," I said. "There will be plenty of Magic before this season's over."

And there was. Within two weeks—after we'd won four of our first five games—my biggest headache was that I was getting too much publicity. I told the guys in a team meeting that I had no control over the press and I hoped all the attention I attracted didn't disrupt the team. Nobody said anything if it did. When we began our Big Ten schedule in January, we'd had only one loss. We ran off a streak of 13 wins before Indiana stopped us at the end of the month.

Midway through the season, the Kansas City Kings contacted my father, feeling him out about the possibility of my turning pro at the end of the season. Although only a freshman, I could turn pro at the end of the year by invoking the NBA's "hardship" rule. All I had to do was notify the league that I wished to make myself eligible for the college draft. It wasn't necessary any longer for an underclassman to prove financial need—as it had been when the "hardship" rule was first instituted.

I was flattered and preoccupied by the feeler for a while, but after discussions with my father and Tuck I decided to deal with it after the season was over. I wanted to forget about it for the time being.

Forgetting about it became difficult, though, once the media got wind of it. Speculation about my future became a popular topic. That's all reporters asked about, even though I repeatedly responded that I'd deal with it after the season ended. I had no idea what I really wanted to do. I felt I could play in the NBA, but I wasn't sure if I wanted to just yet—I was only eighteen years old.

I made the transition to major-college basketball relatively easily, although I had to be careful about getting caught in the air because the college players, being smarter, would back off and play the passing lanes in an attempt to force me to eat the ball. As a guard, I had to adjust to the defense of smaller players, who always seemed to be underfoot. A small, aggressive defender, if he's smart and willing to work, can create a surprising number of problems for a player my size. Most important, I had to adjust to the hard reality of more defeats. My recovery period, once long and painful, became shorter and more tolerable.

We won the Big Ten title outright that season and surpassed twenty wins for the first time in school history. The days of Michigan State having no basketball tradition were over. In the NCAA tournament, we blew by Providence, our first-round opponent. Then we beat Western Kentucky easily to move into the Mideast Regional final against Kentucky, the top-ranked team in the country.

We were a strong, confident team. We were convinced we would not only beat Kentucky but would also go on to take the NCAA championship. Kentucky, we knew, was big, tough, deep in talent, and experienced, but it couldn't match our quickness. As it turned out, Kentucky didn't have to. We took a five-point lead into the half and played cautiously the second, slowing the pace—a strategy that cost us the game. Kentucky beat us by three points and went on to win the championship.

In the locker room after the game, the frustration was everywhere. We felt we'd lost the game, not that Kentucky had won it. Heathcote felt responsible because it was his decision to slow the tempo, taking us out of our rhythm and then the game. He didn't say anything; he didn't have to. He knew he'd made a mistake. Still, we all took pride in our accomplishments. We'd gone further and played better than anybody had expected.

Before my sweat was even dry, I had to turn my attention to the future. For the second year in a row I had a major decision to make. This time: Should I turn pro or not? The NBA's deadline for filing for the college draft was a month away. I thought of reasons for remaining at Michigan State: I was doing well scholastically (on my way to a B average for the freshman year). I loved campus life. I had a chance to be on an NCAA championship team, to be the NCAA Player of the Year (I'd made several All-America teams as a freshman), and to play in the 1980 Olympics.

Yet, I was good enough to play in the NBA, which would fulfill my lifelong dream and give me more money than I'd ever imagined. And I could always return to school during the off-season and eventually earn my college diploma.

While I vacillated, others whose opinions I respected were resolute in their opposition to my turning pro. My mother said it was out of the question—I was too young. My father and Tuck opposed it because they didn't believe the time was right and they weren't sure I was ready. But Kansas City, the team with the NBA's No. 1 draft pick, persisted. By doing so, the Kings aroused my curiosity. I wondered what kind of money they were talking about.

"Tuck," I said to him at his apartment one day, "they've got to be talking about big dollars, don't you think? Big dollars."

"I know it," he said.

"Big."

"Right, big. But what if it isn't guaranteed? Then it doesn't matter how big it is. And if it is, what if you're not ready and you fall flat on your face? You get the money, but you blow the whole opportunity."

"First, there's no way I'd fall flat on my face and you know that."

Tuck nodded. "Yeah, okay, I know that."

"Second," I continued, "if you want to play 'what if,' what if I tear up my knee at Michigan State? Then what?"

This exasperated Tuck.

"What do you want to do?" he asked. "You want to turn pro? Fine, turn pro. You want to stay in college? Fine, stay in college. You tell me."

"I don't know. How much do you think they're talking about?"

"Probably two, three hundred."

"What's my father say?"

"You know what he thinks. He says you're not ready. Let's be real about it. Money is not key. That comes down the line. You'll probably get more next year than Kansas City will give you now. You're not suffering. I have a little change you're welcome to. Your dad has a little change, too.

So, you're not a poor kid. You can't have everything, but you have what you need.

"On the other hand, throw away the Olympics, throw away the possibility of winning an NCAA championship. Those aren't your main considerations. The point is you want to stay at Michigan State because you're having fun. And that's important. You have time, plenty of it."

Nonetheless, turning pro tempted me. "I don't know," I said.

"You want to talk to them or not?" snapped Tuck. "If so, tell me, and I'll set up a meeting. Just you and me. Your dad doesn't want to go."

I hesitated.

"Well, what do you want to do?"

"Okay, arrange it," I said finally.

The Saturday before the Tuesday deadline, we flew to Kansas City to meet with the Kings' general manager, Joe Axelson. We moved carefully to avoid violating NCAA rules. We paid our own way: air fare, hotel rooms, meals, taxis, and all incidentals. While a lawyer or agent was not permitted to negotiate on my behalf, members and/or friends of the immediate family were allowed to join me. Tuck qualified.

Kansas City's initial proposal consisted of a generous annual salary (which was less than what we had anticipated, however), a considerable bonus, and some guarantees.

"That's a lot of money," I said, "but I really think I should go back to school."

They immediately reconsidered and raised the offer. Tuck and I talked, they talked, and the basic figure slowly mounted and eventually leveled off at $250,000 a year for six years. Axelson said that was as high as he could go. I turned to Tuck and told him I'd like to talk privately.

"Let's go," I said as soon as we got outside the door.

"Wait, we can't just go," he said. "We have to give them the kind of respect they gave us."

Inside, Tuck said, "Thank you very much. We really liked the offer. It's fair, but not quite good enough. If something changes, please get back to us."

The telephone lines between Lansing and Kansas City were kept burning over the next few days, but the Kings did not raise the ante. Deadline day came and passed, and I remained at Michigan State.

That summer I played basketball nonstop. I was chosen to play on two all-star teams, one that toured several Southern states and another that toured Europe and Russia. I also toured Brazil with Michigan State.

Pro scouts sat in the stands and licked their chops while watching the workouts that preceded the first all-star tour. Among the players were Joe Barry Carroll, Darrell Griffith, Phil Ford, James Bailey, Rick Robey, Kyle Macy, Sidney Moncrief, and Larry Bird. This team was so tough that Bird, Moncrief, and I didn't start. A player finds out where he stands against this kind of competition. I stood tall with the best of them.

Larry Bird was another one who stood tall, and playing on the same team with him was sweet. There was one game in Atlanta where he and I came down on a three-on-two fast break. I was in the middle. Without looking, I flipped the ball over to him and he immediately responded by flipping it back for the lay-in. The crowd went nuts. No-look passes back-to-back; Larry and I were out there tricking them. Oh, yes, Bird and I were on the second five. But this was a second five that killed teams.

The second all-star tour—to Europe and Russia—was a big one. They rolled out the red carpet for us, so to speak, as representatives of the United States. We practiced in Colorado Springs for two weeks before starting that tour in Europe. Among the players were Griffith, Ronnie Lester, Reggie Carter, Mike Woodson, and our big man, Roosevelt Bouie.

We stayed at the Metropole in Moscow, which is the hotel

in Red Square, and couldn't go anywhere without the company of a few strange-looking dudes. I never carried a camera, but those who did were allowed to photograph only certain things. The people gawked at us even more than the Germans had on my tour the year before. The Russians seemed apprehensive, fearful of approaching us and engaging us in conversation. Nonetheless, it was a fun experience. But I don't think I'd want to live there.

The final game against the Russian national team tarnished the trip somewhat. We got jobbed by the referees. We played well throughout the tournament, and the crowd really got excited over our fast-paced game. They even cheered for us, which felt good. But the last game erased all the good feelings. The referees just cheated. They made some ridiculous calls at the end and gave the Russian team the win by a couple of points. I guess there was no way we were going to beat a Russian team in Russia.

From there I touched down briefly in Lansing before taking off for Brazil to barnstorm with Michigan State. We played six games in six different cities in seven days. I returned from Brazil exhausted. School started in a week, and I wondered what had happened to my summer vacation.

The season began with a media barrage even larger than the one the previous year. Besides local and Detroit coverage, the national press turned its attention to Michigan State in general and to me in particular. I made the cover of *Sports Illustrated* for the first time. To represent the overall classiness of college basketball, I wore a tuxedo, top hat, patent leather shoes, cummerbund, and a big smile while tipping in a basket. Michigan State ranked seventh in the Associated Press preseason poll and was picked by some experts to go all the way.

College had been a dream world the first year. But in January of this second season, that world started to crack. I am a vocal player. If I have an idea, I express it; if I don't understand something, I seek an explanation; if I don't think something will work, I speak my piece. In practice, I never let up—I play to win all the time. Heathcote knew all this when he recruited me, just as he knew I'd always follow his instructions to the letter. All through the first season, he'd let me speak my piece. He'd go along with my ideas sometimes and other times he'd just shut me off. That was fine so long as I had a chance to express myself.

During the second season, though, a communications gap opened between Heathcote and the players. After winning the first two games in the Big Ten, we lost four of the next six, the last an embarrassing defeat to Northwestern. I was frustrated and depressed. I knew we were better than our 4–4 record, but I didn't know what to do about it. I didn't feel I could go to the coach, which really bothered me.

Dr. Tucker tracked me down one morning after the defeat by Northwestern. I'd taken most of the heat for that one, and Tuck had been calling me a couple of times a day to ask how I was doing and make small talk. I kept telling him everything was fine, blah-blah, but he knew differently. Just as my father knew differently. I had dinner at home one night and was unusually quiet. I even turned down my mother's sweet-potato pie, which is the best in the state of Michigan. She was shocked.

"Okay, Junior," she said, "what's wrong?"

"Nothing."

"There's something."

I just shook my head. Meanwhile, I felt my father's eyes burning a hole through me. He watched me all through dinner.

"Don't hold it in," he said.

"It's nothing, really."

"The team worrying you?"

"Nope."

He reached into his hip pocket and pulled out his wallet. As difficult as it was to raise seven children, he had it together enough to keep a roll of bills for show. Of course, he and my mother often went without to allow the children a little more.

He was generous with his money. When I'd gotten into college and knew it was only a matter of time before I turned pro, I'd begun hitting him up for loans fairly frequently.

"Dad," I'd say, "can I borrow some money? I got a date."

"How much you need?"

"Fifty dollars."

He'd take out his wallet and pull out the roll. Before he could peel off the fifty, I'd spot one of his hundreds.

"Why don't you just give me the hundred so I don't have to come back so soon?"

"Hey, that's a lot of money."

"Don't worry, you'll get it back."

Now the table was quiet as my father started thumbing through his roll.

"You need some cash?" he asked.

"No," I said, "I'm all right."

He looked up, surprised. "Something *must* be bothering you."

So when I saw Tuck walking towards me the next morning, grinning from ear to ear, I knew he had been talking to my father. He wore sweats and sneakers, as he usually did. Jenison Field House, a sturdy relic from the 1930s, was deserted at this early hour. The bouncing of the basketball echoed off the brick walls.

"Magic Man," he said as he strolled over.

I grunted in acknowledgment and continued shooting. He rebounded and passed it back. I took a few more shots, then it was his turn to shoot and mine to rebound. Once he had warmed up, he challenged me to a game of one-on-one. We played a tough, hard game, harder than usual, but in the end Tuck was no match for me on this day. I let off some of the steam that had been collecting inside.

"I hope you feel better," he said after the game.

"A little," I said. "You been talking to my father?"

He nodded.

"What's he say?"

"He's concerned."

"You concerned, too?"

"Some," he said. "I'm concerned that you're putting too much pressure on yourself. Despite what the sportswriters are writing, it's not all your fault that the team's playing badly, just as it's not all your doing when the team's winning big. You're good, but you're just one guy.

"And because you're so good, you have to learn how to use the other guys and make them better players. Get them more involved, put some of the burden on them. Maybe Jud can't communicate it, but that's what he's looking for you to do. He wants to work with you, believe me, because he's smart enough to recognize what you can do for him. And if you've got something to say, there's nothing wrong with saying it. But sometimes you have to do it diplomatically.

"Few people know and understand you the way your dad and I do. Being talented is one thing, and being honest is another. But being both sometimes scares people. They don't want to believe it and tend to suspect selfish motives when you suggest something should be done for the good of the team."

Soon after that, Heathcote called a team meeting. Just at the right time. He encouraged everybody to speak, which sparked a lively and productive session. We discussed the communications gap, our poor rebounding, our poor running game, and our tendency to sit on leads while trying to force teams out of their zones. Heathcote made one lineup change, moving forward Ron Charles to the bench and replacing him with Mike Brkovich, a good perimeter shooter who Heathcote hoped would loosen the zone defenses.

We pledged ourselves to salvaging the season. We hoped to sneak into the NCAA tournament, but if that didn't happen, then we'd aim for the NIT. Most important, we decided to turn it out and run. I was ready and eager to go.

The meeting eased the tension. It was winning time, and we played like it. Four games off the conference lead at the time—behind Ohio State, the leader at 8–0—we ripped off nine consecutive victories before dropping the final regular season game to Wisconsin. We didn't feel too bad about it. Our 13–5 conference record was good enough for a share of the Big Ten championship and another trip to the NCAA Mideast Regionals.

This was our chance, probably our only chance. Greg Kelser, the All-American forward, was a senior and would be gone the following season. There was a strong possibility that I would leave as well. We were peaking at the right time. We were primed for this tournament.

We needed five straight wins. First up was Lamar, a surprise winner over Detroit in the first round. We blew by them. But Jay Vincent suffered a stress fracture in his foot, and that hurt all of us. We weren't long on depth.

We moved on to the regional semifinals and finals in Indianapolis, where we knocked off Louisiana State in the semis to set up the showdown against Notre Dame. We wanted Digger Phelps so badly we could taste it. When you play Notre Dame, you play Digger. As head coach, he makes sure he's the whole show.

The game started with a set play. Greg, who jumped center, tapped the ball in front to me. Without looking, I batted the ball over my head to Brkovich, who grabbed the pass on the run and took it in for the dunk. That set the tone, and we beat Digger by twelve to win a trip to the Final Four in Salt Lake City. Joining us were Penn, our first opponent; DePaul, the second-ranked team in the country; and top-ranked and undefeated Indiana State, Larry Bird's team.

After Tuesday's practice, Jud told us we would be leaving the following morning. The first game wasn't until Saturday. But Jud wanted to get us out of Lansing because he didn't like the cocky mood on campus. He feared overconfidence. As a result, we arrived in Salt Lake City two days before the other three teams.

There wasn't much to do there. Wednesday night we went to a movie. The following night a wealthy fan rescued us by inviting the entire team to his chalet in Snowbird, a ski resort outside the city. It overlooked the raw beauty of the snowcapped mountains and deep valleys. A gourmet cook, he turned out a delicious meal that was the highlight of the evening. It was a serene and pleasant break from the pressures of basketball. Then, the next day, Friday, we were back at it. We practiced hard, ate dinner as a team, and turned in early.

Penn was no competition. We led by 33 at halftime and won by 34, the biggest blowout in the history of the final round of four. Indiana State got a 1-point victory over DePaul in the other semifinal. If DePaul could come that close, we knew we could take Indiana State.

Many newspapers the next day surprised us by picking Indiana State. Reporters theorized that we would not be prepared for a good team like Indiana State because we had not been tested in the playoffs. They overlooked the fact that we'd buried our opponents because we were good. Besides, we were acquainted with pressure; five of our six losses during the season had come at the buzzer.

Offensively, our strategy was simple: Run when possible and spread out their man-to-man defense when forced into our set pattern. On defense, we played one of Jud's special zones, a 3–2 match-up zone in which Bird was always hounded by a man and a half. With Bird effectively caged— he shot 7 for 21 from the field—we took control from the opening tip and controlled the pace most of the way. Indiana State threatened briefly by cutting our lead to 6 points with ten minutes to play. But we soon pulled away again to win by 11. It was sweet, real sweet for Jud, Greg, and the guys, in light of our problems in January. A few seconds before the final buzzer, Greg and I embraced at midcourt. "You're one bad dude," I told him.

I was drained that night. I spent some time at an alumni gathering and then joined my parents for a nice, low-key evening along with a few other players and their parents. The next day was celebration time. A huge pep rally was held in our honor in Lansing. The students and fans who jammed Jenison Field House went wild. They surrounded us, cheering us and stomping like mad. From a makeshift platform in the middle of the floor, each player was introduced to the crowd. Jud and the starters were called to speak. When it was my turn, the chant began: "Two more years! Two more years!"

Cheerleaders turned somersaults in front of the platform. The students screamed and clapped. It was college life at its best. As I smiled and held up my hand to stop the cheering, the crowd yelled even louder. It seemed that the more I smiled the more they screamed. I laughed and turned away. Finally, the noise subsided.

"We had a mission to do and we accomplished that mission," I said.

More cheers.

"I don't know about two more years," I continued. "I don't know what I will do, but whatever it is, I hope you continue to support me."

The cheers rang on.

But the ring of the cheers doesn't last forever. Not when your team is in turmoil—as the Lakers were during the middle of the 1981–82 season.

7

Another Day, Another Controversy

MID-SEASON—1981–82

February 3, 1982

There was an uneasy quiet in the Laker locker room to-night. And a lot of smoke from Pat Riley's cigarette. Riley had entered moments before with a scowl on his lips and fire in his eyes. He'd lit a cigarette to calm himself, and now he slowly scanned the room, going from player to player, challenging each with a glare. Each player, in turn, averted his eyes. I leaned against my locker, my arms folded against my chest, and stared blankly across the room.

"Chickenshits," Riley muttered as he took a deep draw on the cigarette. He turned away in disgust and started pacing in front of the blackboard. Pacing and smoking. Smoking and pacing. Head down and thinking, searching for the right words, and gearing himself up for the talk. Since joining the Lakers, I have seen him go from nonsmoker to casual smoker to full-time human chimney.

117

Some coaches have hair triggers on their emotions and blow sky-high over incidental infractions. Players eventually grow hardened to such outbursts. Riley, who was named permanent head coach two weeks after succeeding Westhead, is more judicious in venting his anger. As a former pro, he knows that too many explosions can make a coach the butt of locker room jokes. So when he uses his anger, it's no laughing matter.

Riley was a University of Kentucky All-American and a first-round draft choice of the San Diego Rockets in 1967. He played nine years in the NBA, including five and a half with the Lakers, before bad knees forced him to retire. He had a brief career as Laker broadcaster Chick Hearn's color commentator before becoming Westhead's assistant coach. He worked hard and learned quickly, and eventually made important contributions in the areas of scouting and day-of-game preparation. Riley integrated his television experience into his coaching method. He'd produce videotape sequences of first-half action for halftime analysis and put together individual tapes for each player to take home and study. After the firing, he remained fiercely loyal to Westhead, which was the right thing to do.

As a fringe player, Riley had learned to subordinate his ego to the stars in order to survive. Experiencing the game from the bottom up, he also learned a lot about players' insecurities and how they ache to know what's going on and why. So, as coach, he communicates with everybody, from the first man to the last. If he decides to make a move, he tells the players involved what it is and why he's doing it, so they won't go home wondering if they're messing up. Furthermore, he makes himself accessible to the players' suggestions and ideas.

Riley is young and handsome and normally a study in cool, a man who wears expensive Italian sports jackets and shoes, custom-made slacks and shirts, monogrammed cuffs, stylishly greased hair and wire-framed eyeglasses. Usually, he is Good Old Riles, who believes we know what has to be

done as professionals and allows us "the space"—his term—
to do it. His coaching philosophy is "freedom with control."

But the man wearing out the floor tonight wasn't Good
Old Riles, nor was he cool. He was a coach with serious
business on his mind. There were no smiles or wisecracks
behind his back. Everybody waited for him to speak.

What a season, I thought. We still had half a season to go,
and I was emotionally drained already.

This was turning into a particularly bad day for me. I had
waked up with a sharp pain in my lower back. I wasn't even
sure how it happened, only that it must have been during
the Golden State game the night before, when we blew a
big fourth-period lead and lost on two free throws by Joe
Barry Carroll with no time left on the clock. It was a bitter
defeat, one that put everybody in a bad mood.

My back still hurt this evening as I arrived at the Forum
for a game against the New York Knicks. I wasn't sure if I
should try to play. I was upset—and I hadn't even heard
about all the fireworks.

The fireworks were what had Riley raging in the locker
room. He was furious about quotes attributed to me and
Mike Cooper after the loss to Golden State. I was quoted as
having said, "We run what the coach calls. He was calling
plays for the Big Fella." Coop's quote was, "It's like Kareem
is the only one on this team who can score. We're always
calling plays for him." Riley, angry to begin with, interpreted these quotes as direct attacks on Kareem. I'd been upset
by the loss as well as by my own play, and all I'd done was
answer reporters' questions. I hadn't tried to torpedo Kareem. And I couldn't believe it when one of the ball boys
told me that a broadcaster on a Los Angeles radio talk show
had reported that Kareem and I hated each other and that
an explosion was imminent.

The ball boy told me this as I entered the Forum through
the tunnel entrance. I just laughed it off. I was more concerned about my sore back. Kareem was in the locker room
when I entered. He's always one of the first to arrive.

"Hey, Kareem," I said while walking across the locker room, "I hear I hate your guts."

Kareem laughed. "I hear it's mutual."

Then I felt the tension. Coop, whose stall is next to mine, looked upset. I asked him what was going on, and he told me about the newspaper articles. He had talked to Riley earlier in the day and said that Riley was livid.

Oh, brother, I thought, here we go again.

Dr. Robert Kerlan examined my back in the training room and told me to take the night off. He said it wasn't serious—all my back needed was rest.

The loss to Golden State, the newspaper stories, the mood of the team, my back. Depression set in and took up house as I sat on my stool waiting for Riley to speak. I was the only one in street clothes. Everybody else was in uniforms or warm-ups.

The players' stalls face one another in the locker room. From where I sat, I faced Eddie Jordan, Norman, Kareem, Silk, and Bob McAdoo. Riley and the blackboard were along the left wall. The training room was behind the right wall, the showers behind McAdoo's end stall. Coop was on my left and Kurt Rambis on my right.

I looked over to Riley just as he took one last drag before stamping out the cigarette. He stared at the team.

"Do you know what you're doing?" he said. His voice was harsh, the words angry. He looked around the room again. Nobody said a word. There weren't any volunteers to answer the question.

"You are setting yourselves up for failure just as surely as I'm standing here. You're doing it right now. This minute. You're taking the foundation of the team and knocking it apart with sledgehammers."

Riley paused to light another cigarette.

"As soon as adversity hits, as soon as you lose a couple of games, you start crying and pointing fingers at each other. Shit! Champions, my ass.

"You know why you lost the championship last year? You know why? Because of this. Because players started popping off in the papers about other players. It fomented discontent and unrest. If you want to lose, that's the way you do it. It never fails. Start sniping away behind one anothers' backs like a bunch of college girls.

"But if you want to win, you have to be like this."

He raised his fist, clenching it tightly and squeezing until it quivered.

"You have to be tight. I'm not saying you can't express your feelings and opinions. I'm just telling you to think before you speak. And I'm also telling you to look within yourself before you speak. Maybe so-and-so screwed up, but maybe you screwed up, too. Maybe you screwed up worse. Everybody screws up, for Christ's sake, but we screw up as a team just as we do things right as a team. If something's wrong, or if somebody's screwing up too much, then we deal with it right here, among ourselves, and make it right.

"I don't think I ask too much of you guys, but I do ask one thing. No, I demand one thing. I demand that you accept and adhere to universal truths. I'm talking about right and wrong. And you all know right from wrong. For one player to chastise another player in the press is a universal wrong. If it ever happens again, it will be dealt with as severely as possible."

The room was absolutely still.

"Are there any questions?"

"All I want to say," said Cooper, "is I was misquoted. I wasn't trying to start anything. I don't know where that came from."

Riley nodded, then looked at me.

"What about you, Magic?"

"All I said was, I run what the coach calls," I told him. "I wasn't jumping on Kareem. If I did something wrong, I apologize."

"You know, Riles," said Kareem, "people get misquoted

and things are taken out of context all the time. I don't believe anybody was trying to lay anything on me. These guys are with me." Then Kareem, his arms spread wide, looked around the room. "Isn't that right?"

Guys nodded. I said, "Yeah, that's right. I'm not starting anything."

That was the last thing on my mind. I just wanted to stand in the background and keep away from all the controversy. I already had had enough.

The media reaction following Westhead's firing had rocked me. It was unbelievable. It portrayed me as a big baby—cruel, contemptible, selfish, inconsiderate, petulant, power-hungry. You name it, I was it. And all of this was based on a misconception. I never said, "Either I go or the coach goes." There was no ultimatum, nor was one implied. As many athletes in professional sports had done before me, I expressed my discontent and asked to be traded. That's what I said and that's what I meant.

Cynical members of the media wouldn't accept that. Nonsense, they said, your intentions were clear. They pronounced me guilty of overthrowing the coach. The smoking gun was my contract. They said it prohibited Buss from trading me. But they were wrong. A trade can always be arranged, and Buss, being the innovator he is, certainly could have figured one out. And if my contract stood in the way, I would have torn it up. I was willing to do that during the summer when Kareem questioned if I was part of management.

I guess I was naive, but I really thought the mess would be cleared up as soon as Buss explained he had previously decided to replace Westhead. But instead of putting out the fire, the explanation fueled it. People refused to believe Buss's statements. Some came right out and called him a liar.

"The only thing I could have done differently was not to fire Paul," Buss said. "And had I not, it would have been for only one reason—namely, because of what Magic had said. Therefore, by not firing Paul I would have been guilty of allowing Magic to affect management decisions, the precise crime I was accused of committing for firing him."

Tuck had flown in from Lansing the morning after Paul was fired, meeting me at the team shoot-around. We spent most of the afternoon discussing the possible repercussions, the most immediate being the reaction of the fans that night. We were to play San Antonio at the Forum, and I expected to be booed.

Tuck and I spread out in the living room of my apartment, each with a quart of orange juice.

"Well, how heavy's it going to be?" I asked.

"I don't know," he said. "Could be bad. You have to realize everybody's not going to love you. Most are day-by-day people anyhow, and they don't get into it much. Then you have those who get into your face. They will be the ones booing. But they come and go like the wind. Once that ball starts dropping, they'll be back cheering you."

"Oh, man," I sighed.

"Oh, man, is right. You put yourself into a tight spot."

"What do I do?"

"I'm not going to tell you not to think about it, because I think you should. There's a lot of pressure on you. But once the game starts, you'll have an opportunity to get rid of it. Get the ball to the players—to Kareem, over to Kupchak, make sure Nixon is involved, get Silk the jumper where he likes it. Make sure everybody's involved. All you do is pass, pass, pass the first quarter. If you have an open shot, take it, just don't go looking for it. Your first priority is to get the team moving. It's very important that it gets off to a fast start."

I closed my eyes and thought for a moment.

"I got it," I said. "But what about the boos? How do I handle them?"

"You have to play right on through them."

Knowing it was going to happen didn't prepare me for the actuality of it. Deep down, I prayed they wouldn't boo. I thought, No, these are my fans. Somewhere else, maybe. Not here. They know me better.

My stomach tightened into a knot as the public address announcer began introducing the starters. When it was my turn, I murmured to myself, "Please, don't boo." Despite the plea, the boos started as soon as my name was called. The fans booed long and hard. As I stood in front of a capacity crowd of 17,505, I bit the inside of my cheek to keep my composure and fight back the tears. I'd been booed before. But for the first time the boos were personal and not simply because I was the star of a visiting team. It hurt.

Later that night we turned on the fast break, and the boos turned into cheers. But the pain lingered. It became an unpleasant part of life I had to deal with. I realized I had triggered a complex emotional reaction to issues dealing with money and power.

At the root of it all was the contract. The fan in the street couldn't relate to it—the numbers were too big. He couldn't comprehend how any athlete could be worth $1 million a year for twenty-five years, let alone a twenty-two-year-old kid. I don't know how you determine a man's worth, but I do know the athlete is subject to the same laws of supply and demand as everybody else. The athlete is an entertainer. Every time he goes out to play his game, he performs for the entertainment of the people who pay to watch. Whether he entertains them with the skyhook, or a Norm Nixon jumper, or a slam dunk or a great pass, an athlete should make what he can.

When Westhead got fired, it gave the fan an opportunity to get the boos out of his system. He saw the firing as an example of misplaced power, as proof that the lunatics were running the asylum. But even if I could have the power, I wouldn't want it. The power begins with the owner. He delegates it to the coach. The salary structure is incidental to the interreactions between coach and player. The players recognize the coach's authority and will listen—or not listen—to him regardless of whether he makes more or less money than they do. The bottom line once again is production. If the coach doesn't like a player's production, the coach can exercise power in several ways, one of which is to bench the player. If the owner is unhappy with the results, he can exercise his power as well. One of *his* options is to fire the coach.

The only time the fans booed me at home was the first night. But the road was another story. Some places were worse than others. The worst was Seattle. In a game against the Sonics in the Kingdome exactly two weeks after Westhead had been fired, more than 20,000 people booed me every time I touched the ball. Through the entire game. That blew me out. Every time. When the Seattle fans started, I just shrugged it off. I'd been hearing boos for two weeks and had learned how to block them out and play right through them. But this night the booing wouldn't go away, and it affected my play—I didn't want any part of the ball. It was my worst game of the year, and, to make the evening a total disaster, we lost by six points.

I was exhausted afterwards. I leaned against my locker and just closed my eyes. My teammates knew I had gone through an ordeal. Several asked if I was all right. I nodded. Jerry West, who was about to step down as assistant coach, came over. (That day, the front office had announced that Riley would coach the rest of the season and that a permanent assistant would replace West within a few days. They were in the process of hiring Bill Bertka.)

West pulled up a stool and sat down. "You've got to be strong," he said.

I nodded. "Magic Jackson," I said.

"What's that?"

"I was just thinking about the other day," I said. I turned

to West and smiled. "Reggie Jackson came into the locker room with Dr. Buss after the game and shook my hand. It was the first time I had ever met him. 'I know how you feel,' he said. 'I was driving down the highway when I heard about it on the radio and the first thing I wanted to do was find a telephone. I wanted to call and tell you to hang in there.' I thought that was nice of him. And I told him that a friend of mine had started calling me Magic Jackson. Reggie loved that."

West laughed. "Pretty soon," he said, "they'll be calling him Reggie Johnson."

I kept up a brave front those first few weeks, but it wasn't easy. I had trouble sleeping, my appetite diminished, and I must have kept the telephone company in business with all my long-distance calls to Lansing. When I'm down, I have a tendency to go straight to my home people—to my dad, mother, brothers, and sisters, and to Tuck. They're the ones who bear the brunt of my unhappiness. I feel secure in the knowledge that I can lose control with them, maybe say something nasty, something I really don't mean, and not have to worry about it coming back to me.

I dreaded picking up my mail at the Forum. Mary Lou Liebich, the Lakers' secretary, would frown and sadly shake her head whenever I'd stop by. She'd always have a large packet for me, the contents of which had ceased being fan mail.

"Shall I send it to Lansing?" she'd ask.

"Please," I'd say, "I don't even want to see it."

The packets were sent to Tuck, who would turn them over to my mother. They got rid of the real bad letters. In those days, there were plenty.

Being the heavy. Wow! I wasn't ready for it. My father supported me all the way. But the one thing that bothered him was the lack of public support from my teammates. Privately, they were in my corner; publicly, they didn't want any part of the controversy. I understood where they were coming from and didn't blame them.

"If they weren't satisfied with the way the team was going, they should have been big enough to say something about it," my father said during one long-distance conversation. "They should've said, 'This system is killing us. We're winning, but we're really not winning.'

"If you do something I don't like, I'm not going to go around and around about it," my dad said. "I'm not going to talk behind your back. I'll tell it to your face and get it over with. I'm not going to dwell on it and stay mad. That's how you get in trouble."

"They don't want to get involved," I said. "Besides, it's done with."

"Yeah, it's done with, and you're out there all by yourself. All they have to say is that they shared your frustration. They're professionals. Why don't they act like it?"

I tried to explain that pro basketball is an uncertain business. The public's perception of an athlete's character can be more important to an athlete's career than his ability. And once a bad reputation is formed, it tends to stick. The fact that the reputation is unjustified, as some are, makes no difference because the perception is set. It's crazy. Somehow fiction becomes fact.

A classic example is Bob McAdoo. Throughout the mid-1970s, he was one of the best players in the league. As the center for the Buffalo Braves, he led the league in scoring three straight years, and in 1976 he was named the NBA's Most Valuable Player. Although the Braves never won a division championship, they had winning records and made the playoffs in each of those three seasons that McAdoo led the league in scoring. During those years, nobody called him a loser or questioned his character.

Six years later, following a couple of injuries and a succession of unfortunate trades to teams with bad situations, McAdoo was perceived by the public and the media as a loser, an unconscious gunner, and a malingerer. His reputation was so bad that at age thirty, which is prime time for the great players, nobody wanted him. McAdoo turned out to be one of the lucky ones. He got a chance to prove himself. He knew it would be his last.

He got his chance with us. We needed a backup big man badly, and in December, McAdoo was one of the players being considered. The first time I heard McAdoo's name mentioned was at Pip's, a fancy private club in Beverly Hills. Riley, some of the guys, and I were there as guests of Dr. Buss following a Sunday night game. Riley asked each of us our opinions of McAdoo. I was skeptical. I had met Bob, but I didn't know him. All I really knew was the reputation. When Riley came over to me, I rolled my eyes.

"I don't know if he's what we need," I said. "I think we need a banger, not a scorer—somebody like the Whopper."

The Whopper was Billy Paultz, a big, tough, smart veteran, who was the prototype backup center. He'd had a good season with the Houston Rockets the year before, but he wasn't seeing much playing time this season. Riley liked him, too.

"We can't get Paultz," Riley said. "Houston wants too much."

"Well, if McAdoo can fit in." I paused for a moment. "That's the big thing."

Of all the players, Kareem was the most supportive. He told Riley that McAdoo would be great if he could play.

We signed McAdoo the day before Christmas. By then, I felt I had survived the immediate fallout from the Westhead explosion. People still booed on occasion—some even taunted me from the stands—and a few writers continued to fire their shots, but I no longer experienced widespread hostility. Wherever I went—to dinner, the movies, the bank, the supermarket, the ice cream store—people stopped me to say hello and get my autograph. My life returned to normal, more or less, helped along by the exciting and successful basketball the Lakers were playing.

Riley, perhaps having learned from Westhead's mistakes, unleashed us as soon as he took over. He made several immediate adjustments in the play-sets to create greater flexibility and maneuverability, which resulted in more fast breaks. And he released the tension by opening up the lines of communication.

The end of November and all of December was one long emotional joyride. We won 17 of 20 games, including six in a row without Kareem, who jammed an ankle, and the last five of those without Mitch Kupchak, who suffered a much more serious injury. In a game in San Diego two nights after Kareem got hurt, Mitch took a long pass, then planted his foot awkwardly while driving to the hoop. He charged into one of the Clippers and immediately crashed to the floor, clutching his knee in obvious pain. Everybody's head dropped. This one was serious. I thought, Oh, man, he's down. What are we going to do now?

Mitch had a triple injury—a chipped bone behind the knee, torn cartilage, and a torn ligament. The ligament was the worst part. It's an injury from which some players never fully recover. We all felt terrible.

The next night we played Atlanta at the Forum. I dragged through the warm-ups. Kareem out, Kupchak out for who knows how long? And looking down at the other end of the court and seeing big strong dudes like Tree Rollins, Dan Roundfield, Tom McMillen, and Steve Hawes made me want to cry. Coop read my feelings and tried to perk me up.

"C'mon, Magic," he said. "We need you."

"What're we supposed to do against all those big guys?" I asked.

"Run 'em to death," he answered.

Which we did. Over the next six games we played some of our best basketball of the season. We definitely played our fastest basketball. Referee Earl Strom, who worked two of those six games, stopped me as we broke from a time-out one game. It was a time-out he needed more than we did. "I wish you guys would slow it down a little," he said. "You're running me right out of the league."

I laughed. "It's good for you, Earl."

It was one of those rare times where everybody came together at the same time. We started Jim Brewer at center, Silk and me at forwards, and Norm and Coop in the backcourt. Kurt Rambis made the most of his increased playing time and showed everybody he belonged in the NBA. When a dominating player like Kareem goes out of the lineup, the rest of the guys typically dig in and welcome the challenge as an opportunity to express themselves and make a greater contribution than they normally would.

We sure wouldn't want to go an entire season without Kareem, but it was fun for a few games. I think teams had a more difficult time matching up against this lineup because of our increased speed. Our fast break was devastating. And the more we won, the more we pumped each other up. Nobody was afraid to shoot, not even Brew. If you miss, so what? Get the rebound and make it next time.

Everybody had his moments—Silk especially, by scoring over 30 three times—but the most exciting moment belonged to Coop, whose offense really came on during this stretch. In a game at Portland, he threw down a jam over Calvin Natt that was unbelievable. He went up, and just as it seemed he had reached the top of his leap, he exploded and went even higher. On the dunk, he had his arm up to his elbow in the hoop. The crowd was stunned. Mr. Excitement had struck and you could hear the murmur of oohs and aahs. Time out was called as soon as Coop came down to earth. He stared at Natt in triumph. Calvin probably was wondering what he had done to deserve that kind of treatment.

"I was throwin' it at him," Coop screamed as he came to the bench. He was hyped. You could see it in his wild eyes.

"Ease up, Coop," said Norm, yelling and laughing at the same time.

"In his face," I yelled. "Put it in his face."

"I was trying to hit him," Coop rambled. "That'll teach him to jam on me."

"Talk to him, Coop," Norm continued.

We swarmed all over him, yelling and stroking and hugging and laughing. It was a spontaneous expression of the love that is the ultimate experience in team sports.

Coop finally grabbed a towel and took a seat at the end of the bench. He draped the towel over his head as he does in emotional times and breathed deeply, trying to come down. He was up there awfully high.

What happened after Kareem's return was predictable. All of us were up there awfully high. We had to come down. When we did, we lost our zip. We discovered fatigue, we discovered defeat. On the positive side, we discovered that Rambis could handle the starting forward position and that McAdoo was a good dude after all, even though it was taking him forever to get into playing shape.

Personally, I discovered further controversy. During the middle of our two-week January road trip, newspapers reported that 7-Up was pulling my television commercials off the air. The stories implied that my involvement in the Westhead firing had damaged my image to the extent that I no longer was acceptable to consumers as 7-Up's representative.

I thought—wow!—this is really strange. Seven-Up had signed me right out of Michigan State to take part in its superstar campaign. We had been together a long time and enjoyed a good relationship. I was shocked that they would come out in the papers and smack me before telling me or George Andrews, my attorney. If my image had been hurt and they couldn't handle it, fine. I understand how business works. All they had to do was call George and say, "We have to let him go." *Then* go to the newspapers.

I called George, who in turn called the lawyer for the advertising agency in New York, who then talked to the 7-Up people in St. Louis. The answers made the return trip. My commercials were being taken off the air but not because of my image, they said. Seven-Up was set to begin a new cycle of commercials the next month, and mine, which had had an extraordinarily long life of fourteen months, were being routinely retired. The new campaign had been scheduled long before Westhead was fired. Seven-Up apologized for the flap, which, they said, was caused by one of their executives, who had responded to a consumer's letter protesting my appearance in 7-Up commercials. The executive had written that my commercials were going off the air but neglected to explain why.

Oh my, I thought. George Brett's 7-Up commercials go off the air, Larry Bird's go off, Pat Haden's go off, Mike Schmidt's go off, Dave Parker's go off, Dave Kingman's go off, and nobody notices. My commercials go off, and it's national news. Maybe part of the reason is that I've had more commercials and television appearances than any other basketball player in history.

Not everybody was scared off by the controversy. Al Harden and Joe Dean of Converse and Jacque Hetrick of Spalding stood by me and extended my endorsement contracts, Converse for the rest of my career and beyond and Spalding for two more years. Buick stood by me as well and signed me for a third season.

"Magic, what's all this done to your image?" is a question I've been asked a few thousand times the last few months.

My image has changed, I say. I've been scarred, but I can handle that. It's impossible to go through life without picking up a few scars along the way. So much has happened in such a short period of time that sometimes I forget I'm so young. My image may never be what it was, but it'll still be a positive one. I'm still the same person. My values haven't changed. Maybe the older folks will never forgive me, but the young people understand I'm one of them. They know I'm for them, and that I'm still doing my thing. Kids come up to me all the time to let me know they're pulling for me. They still want me to be the person they can look up to and say, "Yeah, I want to be like him."

One indicator that reflected a shift in my image, if not my popularity, was the fans' All-Star Game balloting. I ran well behind the leading Western Conference guards, George Gervin of San Antonio and Gus Williams of Seattle. The only chance I had of making the team was through the vote of the conference coaches, who select the remaining seven players. Truthfully, I didn't expect much support from them. And I didn't really care if I made the team or not. Either way I was going to party. I was rooting for Norm to make it. The little man was having a great year and deserved to be an All-Star. After he'd put some moves on Isiah Thomas in Detroit, Isiah came up to me and said, "That boy is quick."

"You know that," I said. "Just when you think you have him contained, he explodes on you."

Isiah, Detroit's rookie guard, had put a few moves on Norm, too, which Norm acknowledged. The good pros get into respect. You learn to give it up. Why not? To get to the top you have to have your head together enough to realize and accept the fact that there are players out there who can do sweeter things than you. The dudes who sit up in the stands saying "Oh, he ain't no good" are the ones who don't have it together.

We struggled through the entire month of January. After beginning the New Year with a 20-point loss to Seattle at home, we won 4 of 7 on the road, then 3 of 4 at home. That might be good enough for most teams, but not for the Lakers.

Our last game before the All-Star Game break was a strange one. Phoenix came to the Forum and decided to play a slowdown game against us, even though they'd had quite a bit of success running against us over the years. In this game, they wasted the shot clock almost every time downcourt.

We were surprised. It was as though the Suns were waving the white flag. Some of the Suns were embarrassed. All game Norm called Dennis Johnson "Tar Heel," a reference to North Carolina and its famous Four Corners offense.

"C'mon, D.J., do something," I said while guarding him once. "I'm falling asleep."

D.J. stood about twenty-five feet out, bouncing the ball, and looking at the shot clock. "Just a second," he said. "Twelve, eleven, ten, nine, okay, time to go." And he went. I laughed so hard.

The Lakers were well represented at the All-Star Game in New Jersey January 31. Norm and I were both added to the team by the coaches. Kareem was voted in by the fans. And Riley and Bertka coached the Western Conference team.

It was a good time. The whole thing. The banquet, disco, practices, and even the game, which we lost to the Eastern Conference. While it was hardly a vacation for those involved, at least it was a change from our normal environments.

Two days later—yesterday—we were back in it—in Oakland, losing to the Warriors. And tonight Riley was raging, but to no immediate avail. We lost to the Knicks by four points. It was worse than last night.

I'm upset. I don't like losing. I don't like having a pain in the lower back, I don't like missing a game, and I don't like this latest controversy. I don't know how I got in the middle of it. I don't know if Riley overreacted, or if the press inadvertently interpreted my remarks as criticism of team strategy or of Kareem. I've decided the best way to steer clear of further trouble is to watch my tongue. Which I told the reporters I was going to do after the game.

"Magic," one asked me in the locker room, "is there a problem with you and Kareem?"

"No," I said. "I don't know where that came from. I guess I can't say anything anymore. I try to be honest and say what's going on, and the next thing I know people are saying Kareem and I are at each other's throats. I go out of my way to give as many interviews as possible, and they come back in my face. They create problems for the team that weren't intended. That's not right.

"When I arrived here today, I had no idea what had gone down. I think I'd know if I was in the middle of something. I thought, Here we go again. There's a breakdown somewhere, so I'm just going to have to quit giving interviews if the reporters don't report what I say accurately. Either that, or I'll talk and not really say anything."

The heat is on. We're 7–7 since the first of the year. As Riley indicated at the meeting, Kareem acts as a magnet when the team isn't playing well. Riley showed us a videotape of the final six minutes of the Golden State game and pointed out that only twice had he called for the ball to go in to Kareem. On four other plays, we'd sent it into the post on our own following breakdowns in the offense. Whatever the reasons, we're not running well right now, not creating opportunities off the defense.

During the course of a season, every team goes through its peaks and valleys. We've been in our valley for a long time. Too long. If we stay in it much longer, temperatures are going to roll right off the thermometers. It's time to put up or shut up.

These are the dog days, a part of the NBA I could not imagine while trying to decide whether or not to turn pro after my sophomore season at Michigan State.

8

Breaking Away

Back in college, about a week after winning the NCAA championship, I put on a clinic at one of the boys' clubs. Afterwards, the boys swarmed all over me with their autograph books and little scraps of paper. While signing and talking stuff to them, I felt a tugging on my shorts. I looked down and saw this cute little kid holding on to me. He couldn't have been more than seven or eight, yet he looked so serious. I smiled and put my hand on the top of his head.

"What's the matter?" I asked.

He shook his head and shrugged. He was embarrassed.

"Then why're you pulling on my shorts?" I wiped off my smile, hooded my eyes, and gave him my "mock anger" expression.

He shrugged again. He still looked mighty serious.

"C'mon," I said. Mock anger didn't work, so I softened up and got serious myself. "Tell me what's the matter." I had stopped signing autographs. All the other kids watched and listened.

"C'mon," I said again.

He tilted his head to one side and thought for a moment. Something definitely was bothering him. "Mr. Johnson," he said finally. "My daddy says you're going to leave us. Is that true?"

I mean, I nearly cried. This little boy choked me up in an instant. I looked around at the other kids. They were all staring at me. It was the question all the others had been afraid to ask. The little boy's expression remained as serious as ever. I reached down and grabbed his hand, smiling and shaking my head sadly while doing so.

"Okay, kids. Let's sit down and have a little talk."

The kids, about thirty of them, sat on the dusty gym floor. To the little boy, I said, "You sit with me." I put my arm around him. I remember my words almost exactly.

"First of all," I said, turning to the little boy, "your daddy may be right." Then, I turned to face the group. "But I don't know for sure yet. You all dream about being this or that. Some of you, I'll bet, even dream of becoming famous basketball players. Right?" They all nodded, including the little boy under my arm. "And you want those dreams to come true right away. Right?" They nodded again. "Well, I've always dreamed of playing in the NBA, and I'm lucky because I'm pretty close to having my dream come true.

"But you gotta be careful. You can't just rush into it, because dreams can be deceiving. Sometimes it's not the right one, even though it looks like it. Dreams can be funny that way. So that's what I'm doing now. I'm checking out the dream. If it's the right one, well, I gotta go with my dream."

I smiled. "You boys understand, don't you?" Again they nodded. "But even if I do leave, I'm not really leaving Lansing. I'll just go away for a little while and then come back. I'll always come back, because this is my home and you kids are my people."

Everybody in town, it seemed, was speculating about my future during those weeks following our big win over Indiana State. And I just kept saying "I don't know," which was true. I was playing the waiting game.

I felt, and my father and Dr. Tucker agreed, that the time was right to turn pro. From a financial standpoint, it was perfect. My market value was high, having risen significantly in the last year. It was very unlikely it would again increase that much in one year, or even come close to that kind of increase. And, even if there was a chance that my market value would go up, the risk of injury made that too great a gamble.

Also, creatively, I had put college basketball behind me. There wasn't much left to accomplish, except perhaps win another NCAA title, which was by no means a sure thing, and wait for the 1980 Olympics and possibly a Gold Medal. Moreover, there was no doubt in my mind that I could play in the NBA.

But drawbacks did exist. My mother firmly opposed my leaving school. She argued that I could always play pro ball.

"If you go now," she'd say, "you'll never finish up with school."

"But, Mom," I'd say, "I can take courses every summer. There's no law that says you have to get your degree in four years. I'll get it. Don't worry."

"That's what you say now. But I know differently. As soon as you get some money in your pocket, you'll figure you don't need college anymore."

"I promise I'll get my degree. Man, I don't even know if I'm going to turn pro yet."

"You have to realize, Junior, that you can't play basketball all your life. Right now, that's all you care about and you can't see past it. But getting a college education is one of the most important things in a man's life and I'd hate to see you throw it away. Someday, when you can't play basketball anymore, you're going to wish you had it. I don't think you're keeping that in mind."

She was right. And what's more, education wasn't the main thing on my mind. I was reluctant to leave Michigan State because I was having a ball. I loved it. So in some respects I was ready to leave; in other respects I wasn't. The decision tore me up. One day it would be yes, the next day, no. Ultimately, my decision would depend on the answers to two basic questions: Which team and how much?

Before they could be answered, I had to wait until April 19, 1979, the day NBA commissioner Larry O'Brien flipped a coin to determine which team, Chicago or Los Angeles, would have first choice in the college draft. The Lakers were in the flip because of a three-year-old trade. In 1976 the Jazz, then based in New Orleans, had signed Gail Goodrich, who'd played out his option with the Lakers and become a free agent. In compensation, the Jazz gave the Lakers several draft choices, including their first-round pick in 1979. That was the pick the Lakers were using now.

I knew Chicago wanted me badly, but I wasn't sure about L.A. The league's deadline for underclassmen declaring for the draft was three weeks after the flip.

In the meantime all I could do was wait and wonder and steer clear of all the agents trying to sign me up. About twenty-five contacted me directly; many more talked to my father and Tuck. In light of my trial run in Kansas City, I recognized the need for qualified representation. If I was going to turn pro, a deal would have to be struck *before* the declaration deadline. The negotiating leverage I had was that I could always return to school. I had no intention of giving that up. I needed a lawyer who was good and fast.

According to NCAA rules, I was allowed the use of legal counsel for the sole purpose of interpreting negotiations and contracts. For example, the attorney could discuss legal clauses with both parties and explain to me in layman's terms the items being negotiated. But under no conditions was he to take part in the actual discussions of dollars and cents.

I also wanted the lawyer to be capable of providing a full

range of legal services. I didn't want somebody who would
draw up the contract, take his cut, and run. I needed a
lawyer to help with long-range plans.

I ultimately settled on George and Harold Andrews of the
law firm of Andrews & Andrews in Chicago. Harold,
George's uncle, and George came highly recommended to
me by Gus Ganakas and those athletes who had done business with them. In addition to their sports-law practice,
Harold and George had a law practice with an emphasis on
corporate law, real estate, tax planning, and franchising. We
first met at my request at Tuck's apartment. Tuck was
there, but he was in and out of the room using the telephone most of the time. George and Harold told me about
themselves, their business, and discussed ideas related to
sports law, finances, and my future regarding endorsements. They were sharp and forthright, which I liked. I was
especially impressed with the fact that they negotiated for a
number of high-income clients, which meant they wouldn't
be frightened by the kind of money I expected to be dealing with.

"What do you want to do when you're through playing
basketball?" Harold asked me during the meeting. While I
was checking them over, they were checking me. Even
though I might have been considered hot property, they
had their own reputations to protect and wanted to assure
themselves I wasn't a flake who might come back and haunt
them someday. This, to me, was evidence of their profes-
sionalism and sincerity. They weren't in it only for the
money and the glamour.

"I'm a telecommunications major," I said. I thought for a
moment. "Eventually I'd like to get into radio and television. But the business part. I don't want to be an announcer
or anything like that."

George and Harold's philosophy is that a twenty-year-old,
or even a forty-year-old, who gets big dollars for the first
time in his life needs help. They don't think it's right for a

lawyer to say "See you later" once the contracts are signed. The money is too hard to manage if you don't know what you're doing, and subsequently too easy to blow. They believe in establishing a financial game plan for life, which was what I had in mind. But I made sure they understood I would never be a puppet doing a dance for somebody else. I had to control my own life. They agreed, saying it shouldn't be any other way.

I hoped Chicago would win the coin flip because it was closer to home. But L.A. was all right with me, too. Either way it looked like I'd get my chance to play with a big man for the first time. Chicago had Artis Gilmore and L.A. had Kareem. Playing with Kareem, I realized, would be something special. As the day of the coin flip approached, I became impatient. The suspense was driving me crazy.

On the day of the flip, the Chicago Bulls called heads and the coin came up tails, giving the Lakers the No. 1 pick. Jack Kent Cooke, then the Lakers' owner, said I was his choice, subject to working out an agreement. Fine, I thought, now let's get on with it. But it wasn't that easy. Cooke, being a skillful negotiator, made me sweat. He took his time before beginning serious talks. I pretended I wasn't in a hurry, either. Inside, I was dying.

Cooke made several preliminary calls to Tuck to keep the fires burning. He said he would arrange a meeting in Los Angeles as soon as possible. Meanwhile, Tuck told Cooke that I would very much like to be a Laker but would willingly return to school if an agreement could not be reached before the declaration deadline.

My father, Tuck, and I worked out our strategy while waiting for Cooke to call the meeting. The bottom line was: What would make it worthwhile for me to leave Michigan State? The offer would have to exceed the $250,000 Kansas City had offered the previous summer. That was automatic. Next, we decided it should be the highest sum ever paid to a rookie in the history of the league. We also knew that it could go no higher than Kareem's salary—which at that time was approximately $650,000—because Cooke had to work within his own salary structure. Kareem rightfully belonged on top. That was fine. The ceiling gave us plenty of room to roam.

"What do you think the offer will be?" I asked Tuck during one session.

"Do you mean, how much should you be offered? Or, how much will Cooke offer? I hear Cooke is a very shrewd man. You're going to have to be on your toes."

"He's going to have to be on his, too. How much do you think the offer will be?"

Tuck thought for a moment. "I think, after all is said and done, it'll be five hundred thousand. But he won't start off with anything near that. Whatever he offers, we should come back with six."

"Okay. But five hundred is the number. If I don't hear it, I go back to school."

Besides the ability to get it, we also agreed a prime consideration was the ability to protect it. That's where George and Harold came in. I wasn't going to trade away guarantees and no-cuts for bigger but unguaranteed dollars. Since this was my first contract, security was very important. I was dealing from a position of strength, so it didn't matter how smart or shrewd Cooke was. He could try to intimidate me all day and all night, and it wouldn't matter one bit. If the money and guarantees weren't right, all I had to do was drop my trump card: I'd walk away from the negotiations and go back to Michigan State. I'd walked once and could walk again.

By the time Cooke called to arrange a meeting, I was set. George and Harold were retained and already at work on the contract. They had already prepared the clauses we decided were appropriate for a No. 1 pick. During a meeting in Chicago before flying to Los Angeles, they explained to me, my father, and Tuck what to expect in the way of diplomatic warfare. They told us to remain calm, not to take anything personally, and to remember at all times that we held the winning cards—a fact, they said, that Cooke was well aware of. My father was very impressed with George and Harold.

"Isn't this delicious, Earvin?" Cooke asked, when we met at lunch. Cooke, a self-made multimillionaire who made his fortune in newspapers and radio before turning to sports, was sitting at the head of a long rectangular table during lunch in his Trophy Room at the Forum. On the walls were framed portraits of Cooke at various stages of his life, in various poses with various celebrities, and in the act of accepting various awards. He was a handsome, well-dressed, genteel man in his mid-sixties, and he made it a point to mention that all his tasteful business suits were custom-made numbers imported from London's Savile Row. Though small in stature, he presented an imposing image of confidence, power, and wealth. He also possessed a pretty impressive smile himself. He was tough. It didn't take me long to find that out. Nor did it take me long to realize he liked to phrase questions that were easily answered with a simple yes. But to one—"Isn't this delicious, Earvin?"—I replied, "Not really."

What was being discussed was the main course, sand dabs. Cooke had been raving about them since we arrived. He had called his secretary earlier and ordered his "special" for lunch. But I'm not a big fish man, so they didn't excite me much. At the table with us were my father, Tuck, George and Harold Andrews, Jerry West, Bill Sharman, and Chick Hearn. Chick almost swallowed his fork when he heard my answer.

"What?" Cooke said, raising his voice to the proper pitch of astonishment.

Then he turned to Tuck. "Dr. Tucker," he said, "Do you like the sand dabs?"

"I think they're great, Mr. Cooke," he said.

"Mr. Johnson," continued Cooke, "What do you think of the sand dabs?"

"I like them, Mr. Cooke," my father said. "They're good." Cooke turned back to me. "Earvin, do you know that both your father and Dr. Tucker like the sand dabs?"

"They're all right, I guess," I said.

"All right!" he shouted. "All right! They're delicious."

Cooke was always working, even during lunch. Which meant I had to keep working, too. He put on an impressive show. He'd have been a great actor. He was up and down, hollering at me one minute and sweet-talking me the next. The man could really talk. He'd be quoting something out of Shakespeare, and before you realized it, he'd have moved smoothly into a discussion on antique furniture. He'd come up with some obscure quote or fact and say, "Of course, you know that." He knew full well I had no idea what he was talking about. Everybody else around the table would nod knowingly, but I'd tell him I didn't have the slightest idea. Then he'd give me his smile and I'd give him mine.

Cooke and I both realized an agreement had to be reached right away. We'd flown in for the meeting on a Monday morning, and I had to declare no later than the following Friday. We worked all day. At times, we'd all be in the Trophy Room negotiating; other times I'd be in one room with my father and Tuck while Cooke and his people would be in another. We'd each have a copy of the contract, which we'd examine clause by clause. George and Harold went from room to room making the necessary changes and explanations.

After some tough negotiations, we got Cooke to agree to the following clauses, which George and Harold felt I was entitled to as the No. 1 pick in the draft: a no-cut stipulation and fully guaranteed money. All sums would be paid in the event of injury or payable to my estate upon death. Accordingly, at the age of nineteen my financial future and that of my family was secure. Another unique concession they were able to obtain was permission to utilize the Laker uniform in approved, off-the-court commercial activities, which George and Harold felt would be forthcoming and would further enhance my income and popularity. And they were right.

One clause Cooke refused outright was the bonus provision for financing my future college fees. "I'm not paying for your education!" he shouted during one session in the Trophy Room. "I put myself through school. I'm proud of that. If I can do it, then so can you. An education is the responsibility of the individual." He presented a good argument, and we deleted the provision.

The most difficult negotiations involved the basic salary. Cooke offered $400,000, and we countered with $600,000. As the afternoon wore on—we were scheduled to depart Los Angeles on an early-evening flight to Chicago—we were still $100,000 apart. I was tired and getting edgy. Cooke still appeared fresh. Then Tuck got into it.

"What's another hundred thousand dollars to you?" he asked.

"That's a lot of money!" Cooke jumped out of his seat as if he had been shot. "Don't you know that? It takes most men many, many years to earn that kind of money." He pointed at my father. "Ask Mr. Johnson how much money that is. Twenty dollars is a lot of money."

Then he lit into me. "We can win with you and we can win without you," he said. "The Los Angeles Lakers have made the playoffs seventeen times in the last nineteen years. Did you know that, Earvin?"

"No, I didn't, Mr. Cooke." Then I said to Tuck, "Can I talk to you outside for a minute?"

We went into the hallway. "Hey," I said, "I'm going back to school. I don't have to take this."

"It's up to you," Tuck said.

Inside, I stood by my seat and faced Cooke. "I'm ready to go back to school," I told him.

He looked genuinely surprised and upset. "Oh, no," he

said, "don't do that. I would very much appreciate it if all of you remained in Los Angeles as my guests for the night so we can meet again in the morning."

We looked at each other and grimaced. We had wanted to avoid this. We thought we'd accomplish what we had to do in one day. Besides, my father was supposed to be at work the next day. And I knew George and Harold had commitments. Cooke, noticing the hesitation, leaped into the breach.

"Please, I insist. I promise to make it worth your while. Everything will be worked out in the morning. You'll see."

I turned to my father. "What do you think?" I asked.

He shrugged. He wasn't happy about it. "I don't know. If we can finish up . . ."

"I assure you, Mr. Johnson," interrupted Cooke. He stood and smiled brightly at my father. "We will finish first thing tomorrow morning."

"Well," my father said, "if you're so sure we'll finish first thing tomorrow, how come there's a holdup now? Why can't we just go ahead and do it?"

"I wish we could. But please trust me, Mr. Johnson. It's just a minor matter I must take care of."

My father put it back on me. "What do you think?"

"I don't know."

"We may as well stay until the morning, then," my father said with a sigh.

The next morning, following a few minutes of small talk, Cooke got down to business. While the rest of us sat, he stood behind his chair at the head of the table. He wore a gray business suit, white shirt, and club tie. His silver hair was neatly combed and his teeth—on display when he smiled broadly—were perfectly even and white. He oozed confidence.

"I have good news for you, Earvin," he said. "You, too, Mr. Johnson, and Dr. Tucker. Earvin, even though you are only a mere nineteen-year-old lad, I have acquiesced to your wish to become the highest-paid rookie in the history of the National Basketball Association."

He smiled. I smiled back. Everybody was smiling. Well, I thought, he's finally come around.

"I have raised the offer to its limit. Four hundred and sixty thousand dollars." He let the numbers hang for a moment. "Now, Earvin," he continued, "isn't that wonderful?"

I strummed my fingers on the table. I still hadn't heard the numbers I wanted to hear.

"Well, isn't it, Earvin?" he asked again.

"I gotta think about it," I said. I turned to Tuck, stood up, and motioned him outside.

"Earvin," Cooke said softly.

I turned around.

"That is my final offer."

"Okay."

Tuck, Dad, George, and Harold followed me out.

"Should I do this, or what?" I asked my dad as soon as we stepped outside the double doors. Tuck, meanwhile, looked up and down the hallway. The day before, Forum employees had occasionally been wandering around, but now there was nobody in sight.

"You have to make the decision," Dad said.

I turned to Tuck. "What do you think of the money?"

"Hey, let's be real," he said. "Let's not talk about whether the money is right or not, because it's quite obvious that the money is great. Let's not even be concerned with it. Let's talk about you. Do you want to leave school?"

I shrugged.

Tuck continued. "Your mind is in the pros, but your heart is back at school. Which do you want to follow? We've gone through this before. We can walk away again if we have to. It's no big thing. You just have to decide."

We were quiet for a few moments. I leaned against the wall, thinking.

I turned back to Tuck. "The money is good, isn't it," I said.

"Hell, yes," said Tuck. "Plus you got a good franchise here and you'll be playing with the Big Fella. This is a winning situation. If you wait, you may not get one next time."

"What do you think?" I asked George and Harold. They looked at each other.

"I don't think that's his final offer," Harold said.

"If we can get four eighty, we'll do it," I said. "Otherwise, we go home."

"Mr. Cooke," I said when we returned to the Trophy Room. Cooke continued to stand and I stood as well. "We discussed the pros and cons of your final offer and concluded that the smartest thing for me to do is to go back to school for at least another year. So I appreciate everything you've done for us, and I hope we haven't caused you any inconvenience."

"Earvin." Cooke smiled and walked over to a set of mounted photographs on the wall. "Have you seen these?"

"No, I haven't."

"Well, would you like to see them? I'm not going to bite you."

I joined him. He put his arm around me and pointed to several photographs of the Forum, each showing a different stage of the construction. He explained what was in each picture. He was very pleasant. And very proud of the arena he had built in 1967.

"It is a beautiful building, isn't it?" he said.

"It's okay."

He laughed a deep, guttural laugh. "You won't agree with me on anything, will you?" he said. He turned back to the photographs. "I don't care what you think. It is a beautiful building, the best of its kind in the world. And because it is the best, I believe it is only fitting that the best athletes play here. Jerry West has played here. Elgin Baylor has played here. Wilt Chamberlain has played here. Kareem Abdul-Jabbar plays here now.

"And I want you to play here, Earvin. I promised last

night that we would conclude these negotiations this morning. I always keep my promises. I will give you your money."

His face brightened while he made the $500,000 offer. "Is that all right, Earvin?"

I smiled.

"You can say yes now, you know," he said.

"Yes, it is," I said.

"Good." He put out his hand, and we shook on it.

We ate lunch before leaving. This time he let me choose the main course. I requested pizza, which surprised him. He said he had never eaten it before. Nonetheless, he ordered it for everybody. While waiting, he gave me a tour of the building and showed me the original blueprints. He was right. The Forum is a beautiful arena.

Lunch was fun and easygoing. Everybody got along great. Cooke even enjoyed the pizza.

"This is good," he said.

"Yep," I said, "it might catch on."

We laughed about that.

Even though I wanted to turn pro and was sure I would, I still had until Friday to make the final decision. The deal with Cooke was predicated on my declaring for the NBA's college draft. Once I returned to Lansing and to my familiar and comfortable environment, I began having second thoughts. My mother was still dead set against my leaving school. She made me promise to attend summer-school sessions until I graduated.

"Remember you promised, Junior," she said to me. "If you don't finish school, I'll never let you forget it."

I announced the final decision during a press conference at Michigan State on Friday. I was going pro. Students were disappointed, so were people around town, and some of the kids were heartbroken, but nobody condemned me. Everybody knew I had to go pro. Just as I did.

It was time to leave home for a little while.

9

The Happiest Fellas

"Ladies and gentlemen, this is one of the most historic events in Laker history. . . ."

With those words, I was introduced to the people of Los Angeles. I smiled and couldn't help but giggle to myself. But Chick Hearn, who was opening the press conference that was being held to announce my intention to join the Lakers, continued:

"He is like a breath of fresh air, who will breathe new life into the Los Angeles Lakers. . . ."

I sat behind the podium with Jerry West and the general manager, Bill Sharman. West, the Lakers' coach the previous three seasons, had all but formally announced his plans to step down from the job. But, for the moment, he sat there as head coach. West and Sharman, I thought, as I looked the two all-time All-Star guards up and down. Wow! This is the big leagues.

The press conference was taking place five days after the Michigan State press conference and eight days after I'd reached agreement with Jack Kent Cooke. The official announcement here was that the Lakers and I had agreed to agree. The contract would become official as soon as the NBA draft was conducted six weeks later. Although everybody knew, or should have known, that the papers were signed, sealed and delivered, the Lakers, in accordance with league policy, could not make the formal announcement until the draft was over.

"I don't remember a young man in recent years, maybe ever, who has captivated fans the way Magic has," Chick went on.

The Forum press lounge was packed with media people. Dr. Tucker and George Andrews stayed in the background, leaning against the back wall. The Lakers had been criticized for being a blasé team the last few years—ever since West had retired in 1974, actually—and Chick was hyping me as the person who'd warm up the franchise. Attendance in the recently concluded season had been less than 12,000 on the average, which was the team's second lowest figure in eleven years. Chick predicted I would bring in an additional 2,000 fans a game. I hoped he was right. I knew I would try.

Since the NBA did have a "cool" image and several pro players already had been quoted as saying my rah-rah enthusiasm wouldn't work in their league, the reporters wanted to know if I planned to change my ways.

"I'll continue being me as long as my teammates let me," I said. "I'm not going to try to take over or anything like that, but if something's happening and something needs to be said, I'll say it. If my teammate doesn't want to listen, well, then I can't help that. That's me. But I do so to help the team win. That's my main concern."

Then they wanted to know if I would dare make suggestions to Kareem. I gave them my smile. "Do you mean, will I be intimidated by him?" I shook my head. "No. I'll just say, 'Big Fella, would you mind moving over to the other side for a minute? ' " They cracked up, which made me feel better.

I was kind of scared of L.A. at first. The big city and all that. The fast life. Hollywood. The freeways. The smog. But I'd also heard about the crowds. I had heard that fans arrived late and left early, that they rarely cheered or got excited. I couldn't understand that. Why, I wondered, would they bother coming in the first place? Plus, people had told me that the media were vicious and would tear me apart if I didn't come through right away. I wasn't used to that. Back home, everybody's crazy about ball. The fans come out and cheer whether you win or lose. And while the press is tough, it's fair at the same time.

Still, once I decided to turn pro, I felt good about it. One of the first things I did was indulge in a little luxury. I bought myself a nice ride, a Mercedes. So did my Michigan State teammate, Greg Kelser. He was taken fourth in the draft, by Detroit. The two of us cruised around campus those last few weeks of school. It was fun. We were pros, but still students.

Everybody in Lansing, it seemed, wanted to talk to me about the Lakers:

"What do you think it'll be like playing with Kareem?"

"Is West quitting?"

"Who's going to replace him?"

"Will you and Nixon be compatible in the backcourt?"

"What did you think of Larry Bird getting all that money?"

I didn't remain the highest-paid rookie in NBA history for long. Bird had been drafted by the Boston Celtics as a "senior eligible" the year before; the freshman class he'd entered college with had officially graduated that year, but he had dropped out of school for a while and still had another season of college eligibility, which he'd chosen to use. Bird had had even more leverage than I'd had. Where my trump card was that if I decided not to go "hardship," I could return to school and reenter the draft next year, Bird could reenter the NBA draft next month. The Celtics were required to sign him before the draft or lose him. They signed him for about $600,000.

Nor did I remain an employee of Jack Kent Cooke very long. Two weeks after the press conference, Tuck called. "Do you know that some other guy now owns the team?" I told him I didn't. I also didn't think it was too significant. I already had my contract; I was fully protected regardless of who owned the team. Also, I was under the impression that players rarely, if ever, had contact with the owner once the contract was signed. Nevertheless, I was sorry to see Cooke go. I liked and respected him. We'd had a good duel in his Trophy Room.

The first time I met the new owner, Jerry Buss, was the day of the draft at the Plaza Hotel in New York. It was his first official appearance as owner of the Lakers, and he was very excited and enthusiastic.

"I'm the happiest man in America," he said when we met. He did look happy.

"No, you're not," I said. "I am."

Buss laughed. "I think it's safe to say we're two of the happiest men in America."

I laughed and agreed heartily.

While I didn't get a chance to talk with him at length, my parents did and they liked him immediately. They particularly liked the relaxed, everyday quality about him. My father, surprised that he was so easy to be with and talk to, called him a "homebody." It was obvious from Day One that Dr. Buss was a far cry from Mr. Cooke. But at the time I had no way of knowing how very different they were.

We met again about a month later. In addition to playing in various All-Star games around the country, I arranged to play a game in Los Angeles with the Lakers' summer-league team. I spent several days in town to practice with the team. One night, Buss invited me to dinner. It was fun—we talked about everything from basketball to business—and I enjoyed his company. But I wondered about his style of dress. He was dressed like a businessman at the draft. At dinner, however, he was wearing what I later discovered were his everyday clothes: beat-up jeans, a shirt unbuttoned far enough to show some gray chest hairs, and a few gold chains. It was a change for me, but, remembering what my father had said about him, I put all the surface stuff out of my head. I never go on first impressions anyway. And I'm glad I don't, because Jerry Buss is for real all the way. There is nothing phony about him. He worked hard to make his money and decided, when he was in his late forties, that it was time to enjoy it. Which was why he bought the Lakers.

Dr. Buss, Bill Sharman, and Jack McKinney, who would replace West as head coach three days later, were among the sellout crowd packed into the Cal State Los Angeles gym for the game. On normal nights, summer-league games drew two or three hundred people. On this night, there were several thousand and, according to reports, several thousand more were turned away at the gate. I couldn't believe it. I thought I'd create some interest but not so much so soon. It made me realize that the Los Angeles fans were there. They were waiting to be brought out.

Jack McCloskey, the Lakers' assistant coach under West for three years, coached the summer-league team. He called me aside in the locker room before the game.

"Magic," he said, "I'm not going to start you."

"Fine," I said. "No problem with me."

But it was for the fans. You could hear the buzz in the crowd when the starters were introduced. Some people booed when the game began. It was obvious the vast majority had come out to watch me play. But McCloskey, a tough competitor who wants to win every game out, whether it's a playoff game or a meaningless summer-league game, didn't start me because I had joined the team in the middle of the summer season and wasn't familiar with the offense and the players. Again, that was fine with me. I still played twenty-eight minutes, which was plenty of time to get my game going and do a few tricks for the fans. They left the gym happy.

Towards the end of the summer, long after the novelty of owning a new car had disappeared and after the last summer All-Star game had been played, a mild depression set in. I was sad about leaving Lansing. Going to L.A. was much different from going to college.

First finding a place to live and then moving were tremendous hassles. During my last year at Michigan State, a roommate and I had paid $250-a-month rent on an off-campus apartment. Prices in L.A. were out of sight. The identical apartment would have cost four, maybe five times as much. I wanted to buy for investment purposes, but those prices were even crazier. Small condos started at $200,000. Eventually I found an apartment close to the Forum and the airport, where I'd be spending a lot of my time. Leaving home wasn't easy for me by any means. Tuck joined me for a couple of weeks before the start of camp. He liked Los Angeles right off. I don't know how he did it, but he knew enough to show me around town. He took me to a few out-of-the-way spots for some good home cooking. He also helped me furnish the apartment and generally made sure I got my home life together.

The people, I was happy to find out, were super nice. In the lobby of a movie theater one night, I noticed this dude staring at me strangely. I didn't know what to think. So, I just shrugged it off and started walking past him to enter the theater. All of a sudden he started shouting, "That's Magic Johnson!" There was instant hysteria. In a matter of seconds, people surrounded me, wanting autographs and stuff. It really tripped me out.

By mid-September I was over my depression. Training camp was going to begin soon. But I was not entirely over my fondness for Michigan State. I kept thinking that school would be starting in a few days and that I'd already be hanging out with my boys on campus, checking out the new freshmen—and freshwomen. Those were exciting days, I thought.

But so were these. Before going out on the Forum floor for Photo Day that first day, I checked myself in the mirror to see how I looked in my gold-and-purple Laker uniform. On the inside, I was yelling my head off. On the outside, I just looked and smiled.

"Fit all right?" the trainer, Jack Curran, asked as he walked by.

I smiled. "Yeah," I said, "fits perfectly."

"Number okay?"

"Yes."

The number was fine. I couldn't wear 33, my number at Michigan State, because Kareem had it. I wasn't about to tell the Big Fella to turn it over. Thirty-two was just as good, anyway. I wore both numbers in high school and took 33 in college because Kelser had 32.

I was scared the first couple of days. It was like, Okay, I'm here now; it's time to display my talent. Some of the players, as well as quite a few fans, thought the Lakers had made a mistake by drafting me instead of a power forward to fill an immediate need. But it didn't bother me; speculation goes on all the time.

The veterans treated me as I expected they would—as a rookie. They were taking a wait-and-see attitude before warming up to me. They had heard and read all about me. A player can fool the fans and possibly the coach, but he can never fool his teammates. Mine wanted to see what I was made of. So I had to get down right from the start and show them.

I noticed immediately that a much more physical game

was played in the NBA. That and defense are the most significant differences between college and the pros as far as the game itself is concerned. Tuck had warned me about the roughness. I had seen it, but experiencing it was something else. In training camp, where guys are fighting for jobs, you battle every inch of the way. I'm a battler by instinct and adapted immediately. They found out I could play.

Because you no longer play against teams that have one good player and four so-so ones, defense becomes almost impossible. The guys in the NBA are too good and too smart. Once a weakness is spotted, it's exploited to the hilt. If you don't come off picks well, you'll be running into picks all night long. If you don't have much quickness, you're in big trouble all the way around.

But the single most important transition is mental. If a player has the talent, he should be able to make the physical adjustment. Mentally, you never know. That's the big question mark. Suddenly, you're faced by the grind of an eighty-two-game regular schedule, life in a new city, strange faces, loneliness, the media, demands on your time, the hustlers, and the money.

Turning pro allows most guys a chance to splurge a little bit for the first time in their lives. But you have to watch it. Splurging can become an addiction; it can also attract some unwelcome dudes. I splurged by buying the car; I also bought my parents a nice house, which I didn't consider splurging. But that was it. Everything else went straight into the bank or into investments.

I was fortunate to have people like my parents and Tuck backing me while I was growing up. They prepared me mentally in many ways. Besides making me strong, they always made their strength available when I faltered. Having competed against pros since high school, I believed I was prepared for the basketball part as well. I was ready all the way around. And I was champing at the bit in anticipation of the start of the regular season. People kept warning me about pressure—I had gotten so much press, they worried that too much would be expected of me.

"What pressure?" I asked them. "That's okay. I know it's out there, but I don't feel it. I like the idea of people wondering how I'm going to do. The more people wonder, the more people will turn out for the games. That's good for me and the team. If you don't have people yelling and screaming in the stands, then you don't have anything."

By the end of the preseason, I felt like one of the boys, accepted by everybody, particularly by those I was most concerned about, the veterans—Kareem, Norm, Silk, Ron Boone, and Spencer Haywood, whom we acquired for Adrian Dantley in a straight-up deal with the Utah Jazz the day before training camp opened. I beat out Boone for the backcourt position opposite Norm and started opening night against the Clippers in San Diego.

As in high school and later at Michigan State, I had a bad case of the butterflies the night before and the day of the opener. I was terrible the first nine minutes of the game. Finally, Jack McKinney gave me and himself a break. Thoughts of those earlier games made me cringe. I promised myself this one would be different. From that point on I was fine—I settled down and played fairly well. We battled the Clippers uphill all the way and finally beat them by a point on a beautiful eighteen-foot skyhook by Kareem at the buzzer. I was so emotionally charged up I leaped into Kareem's arms and hugged him with all my might. I was so grateful he'd pulled it out for us. My embrace startled him for a moment. Then he broke into a game-winning smile. It was much more than just another game to me.

Somebody else wearing a game-winning smile was Dr. Buss, to whom it also was more than just another game. Over the next few months, Buss and I became very friendly. It was not unusual for him to telephone me on an off day.

"Magic," he'd say. "What're you doing?"

"Nothing," I'd answer. "Watching some television. Probably go out for lunch later."

"If you feel like it, why don't you drop by? We'll shoot some pool."

He also invited the other players to his house—or out to dinner, a disco, a fight, or an ice-hockey game—but few accepted on a regular basis. As veterans, they were unaccustomed to social overtures from the owner and perhaps they were inhibited by his presence. I wasn't. I didn't act any different around him from the way I acted around the players in the locker room. I joined him most of the time because I simply had nothing to do. I was single, didn't know anybody in L.A. other than my teammates, and was reluctant to strike up friendships with strangers. Tuck had warned me about groupies and hangers-on, afraid I'd be an easy mark. By keeping an eye open those first few months, I found myself alone most of the time. Buss, knowing this, gave me a place to go and somebody to talk to, which turned out to be a reciprocal arrangement. As a rookie owner with only a basic knowledge of the game, he was unsure about his ability to run a basketball team. We were two rookies trying to make it at the same time.

"You know, Magic," he said to me once, "I feel that as long as we can talk like this, everything is going well. It's reassuring to me. Because if I were screwing up, I don't think you'd feel comfortable about coming over here."

We never got into team gossip. He wouldn't ask me who was doing what, and I didn't offer. That's team stuff. If something funny happened or if somebody did something outrageous, we might share a laugh over it. When we talked basketball, which wasn't often, we'd talk about games or some of the players around the league. He might ask about a specific play or sequence of plays, which I'd try to explain. But mostly we'd talk about personal stuff—about my family, his family, his youth in Kemerer, Wyoming, and how he had put himself through college hustling pool. He was one straight shooter, but I gave him some good battles. I don't lose easily, not even in pool.

He invited me over to his house the day after the opening game against San Diego. At the time he lived in a large ranch house in one of the canyons on the west side of L.A. This was before he purchased Pickfair, the estate of the silent-film star Mary Pickford. We shot a few games in the paneled billiard room.

"What did you think of Lloyd Free?" he asked while measuring a shot. "Three ball over here." He tapped a corner pocket.

"Whew, that boy wore me out," I said. "Forty-six points."

"What did he shoot? Nineteen for twenty-nine from the field or something?" Click. Buss made the three ball in the corner pocket.

"Nice shot," I said. "Yeah, something like that. He couldn't get enough of me. I think he wanted me to move in with him so he could play against me every night. After he made one from about twenty-five feet, I said, 'Lloyd, you can't be serious?'"

Buss walked to the other side of the table to line up another shot. He put his cigarette on the rail. "Really?" he said. "What did he say?"

"He said, 'You can call me World.'"

Buss looked up and smiled. "Did he really?"

"And I said, 'Anything you say, Mr. World.'"

We laughed. He tapped a side pocket with his cue, lined up the shot, and made another one.

"Kareem's shot was something, wasn't it?" he said while chalking his cue.

"Oh, man, was it," I said. "I'll tell you, that's the prettiest shot ever. He makes it look so easy. That one was from way out there, maybe twenty feet. I couldn't believe it when it went in. Whoosh! The Clippers were stunned, too."

"You sure got excited."

"I couldn't believe it. All game, we're coming and coming

and coming but not going anywhere. Finally, we get ahead right near the end, but lose the lead right back. I'm thinking, Oh, no. Don't tell me we're giving it back after working so hard. I wanted to win so badly, with it being my first pro game. And it looked hopeless. Even after Coop makes the big defensive play to force the turnover. That gives us, what? Three seconds?"

"No, two."

"That's even worse. You know how tough it is just to get a decent shot with two seconds to go, let alone make it? Real tough, believe me. Then the Big Fella moves right in there and swoops for two. I was in heaven."

"I felt a surge of pure happiness," said Dr. Buss. "In fact, I still feel it today. Just thinking about it gives me goose bumps."

He walked around the table looking for another shot. He picked up the cigarette and faced me.

"You know," he continued. "I don't think anybody ever goes into sports figuring he's going to make money. It's possible, but you have to work twice as hard as you would in another business. The motivation is pure and simple—you just really want to have some fun. And today I feel like I'm going to have all kinds of fun."

"That's what it's all about," I told him.

10

A Terrific Mother's Day

PLAYOFFS—1981–82

May 9, 1982

What a great day this was. First, we won the game—beating San Antonio in the opener of the playoff series for the Western Conference championship. Afterward, most of the reporters crowded around Bob McAdoo, their new glamour boy. I was glad to see it; he deserved it. He really started coming on for us towards the end of the regular season. And now, in the playoffs, he's been impossible to stop. This must be the Bob McAdoo of the mid-1970s.

Bob and Coop coming off the bench. Whoa. Double dynamite—Mr. Offense and Mr. Defense. And to think that we've been criticized for having a lack of depth.

In the locker room, I was dressing as quickly as possible. I had a date waiting. Tuck was standing next to me. He was in town for the first two games of the San Antonio series.

"Is this right?" I asked.

Tuck laughed as he inspected my tie, saying, "You'll never get it right." He reached over to fix the knot, and I stretched my neck to give him plenty of room. "Man, you made a mess of this," he said.

I was decked out—slate-gray wool-gabardine suit, white shirt, tie, the works. So was he, in a navy-blue suit.

"Is she bad?" I asked.

"Yeah, she's bad. How many times I have to tell you?"

Tuck had telephoned last night as soon as he arrived in Los Angeles. "I'm bringing a lady to the game tomorrow," he'd said. "She wants to meet you."

"Don't bother," I told him. "I don't need any new ones."

"You won't want to miss this one," he'd said, and I'd said okay.

Tuck has a good eye for women, so I knew she must be special if he wanted to set me up. I knew she didn't smoke, drink, or do drugs. I knew she wasn't married and didn't have a baby. If Tuck says a woman's "bad," that means she's a thoroughbred. After the game, I was anxious to see what she was like.

"How'd you meet her?" I asked as he continued to fix my tie.

"I told you. I met her in Lansing a few weeks ago. She was visiting."

"She knew me?"

He shook his head. "You're crazy, you know that? I told you. She said she'd like to meet you sometime, and I told her I'd be out in a couple of weeks and would take her to a game and introduce you to her."

"What's she do?"

"What do you mean?"

"What's she do? Does she work?"

"I don't know. She's a professional woman or something. Smart."

"You done yet?"

"No, this is no good. I have to start over."

While Tuck untied the knot, I scanned the locker room. A

few reporters were still talking to Bob—or "Doo," as we call him.

There had been a lot of happiness in the room after the game. In beating the San Antonio Spurs by 11 points, we'd reassured ourselves that our momentum was as strong as ever. We'd started the playoffs against Phoenix and swept them in four straight. Then, we'd had a week off. While everybody welcomes a rest, there is always a danger that a prolonged layoff can take a team out of its rhythm. But this afternoon we were sharp.

Kareem had a big game, scoring 32 and blocking 5 shots. Norman had a good game, too. He tore Johnny Moore apart while scoring 31. And Doo, off the bench, scored 21 and played some tough defense. Before the playoffs began, Pat Riley told Bob to expect more playing time. Riley believed Bob would be the key to our success. Nobody his size can match up with him. He's too quick. And that jump shot— what a pretty sight. It's so soft. He shoots it high, with perfect backspin. When it comes down, it just flicks the net.

Bob needed a month and a half to get into game shape after joining us in December. Which was a long time. Then—bam!—he tore a calf muscle in Seattle just when he started playing well and helping out. Nobody rushed him back—there was no sense in doing that. We needed him healthy for the playoffs. He missed three weeks and re-joined us in mid-March as we warmed up for our playoff drive. He stepped right in and hasn't had any problems since.

After the game today, the guys ran into the locker room screaming and slapping palms. We huddled up, put our hands out, one on top of the other. " 'Ray, team!" Five wins down, seven to go. Those were the simple mathematics of winning the NBA championship.

"Doo!" screamed Norm. "I keep telling you. Stick with me and I'll get you that ring."

"What do you mean, stick with you?" said Bob.

Those two boys are something else. They've been ragging

each other for months, cracking everybody up. It's like who can outtalk whom. And I had been under the impression that Bob was a quiet, introspective kind of guy. He's just the opposite. He's a perfect fit on this team.

"Hey, Buck!" Norm yelled across the room. "Didn't I tell him I'd get him his diamond?"

"You know that," I said, laughing.

Bob was sitting on his stool, smiling, the sweat still dripping down his face. "Stick with you, sssshhh. I wouldn't want to stick with you. I can't even see you, you're so small."

"You better look harder, because you've never won anything on your own," said Norm. His face brightened. He turned to me and Coop, laughing and pointing a thumb in McAdoo's direction.

"Nick," Coop said, laughing. "Ease up."

"Little Norm," said Bob. "How many scoring titles do you have? I've won three. And an MVP."

"You gotta diamond? Let's see your diamond. I've got one."

"You couldn't even carry my shoes," said Bob.

Silk, whose locker is next to McAdoo's, started giggling. "Do it, Doo," he said.

"That's ancient history," said Norm.

"How many times have you gone over forty, Little Norm?"

"The diamond. Tell me about the diamond."

"Ask Kareem," Bob said. "It wasn't that long ago."

"Two for McAdoo," said Kareem, laughing.

"Show me the diamond," Norm continued. "I want to see your diamond. That's all that counts."

Norman ended every argument with the same airtight case. There wasn't much Doo could say. All those scoring titles paled in comparison to the championship diamond ring. Winning was all that mattered.

At the moment, though, the lady waiting for me also mattered—some. Tuck finished tying the tie.

"How do I look?" I asked.

"You won't scare her away."

"Where's she at?"

"Forum Club."

"Let's go."

The Forum Club was jammed. Normally, I wouldn't have gone near the place. Everybody, it seemed, wanted to talk to me about the game. I'd smile, say hello, and keep moving.

"Where is she?" I asked.

"Over here," Tuck said. "Just follow me."

I followed him to the rear of the club. Then I stopped short.

"Aw," I said. "What're you doing here?"

Smiling sweetly and sitting alone at a table was my mother. I frowned at Tuck, who was holding his gut to keep from laughing too hard.

"Man, Tuck," I said. Then I smiled; I couldn't help it. I leaned down and gave my mother a big hug and kiss.

"Happy Mother's Day, Mom."

"Thank you, Junior."

"Did you see the game?"

"Yes, I did," she said. "It was so exciting."

I was glad she had seen us play. I was proud of our team and happy to have an opportunity to share my pride with those closest to me. There had been a few rough spots the second half of the season, but they've been smoothed over now. We are peaking at the right time.

After the Golden State game in February and the turbulence that followed, we, as a team, vowed to stop anything that threatened to come between us. If a team beat us, fine. That we could deal with. But we weren't going to beat ourselves. To avoid doing that, we realized we had to take a different approach to team dynamics. Instead of tiptoeing through the locker room, reluctant to express true feelings and opinions for fear of bruising somebody's ego, we said the hell with it. Everybody has an ego, and on this team there are some giant ones. So what. If something has to be said, we decided, say it. We know how far to drive a guy before backing off. As long as mutual respect exists, frankness and honesty work. And we have that. A player's teammates have a better understanding of what makes him tick in most cases than his wife does.

We didn't begin playing consistently well until the middle of March. In February, though, we had a few peaks. Coop was tremendous in a come-from-behind win over the Celtics in Boston, holding Larry Bird to 11 points while scoring 31 himself. Coop's size, speed, quickness, and strength are murder on Larry. Another reason Coop stops him is Coop's frame of mind—Coop enjoys it. It was about this time that Kareem broke out of his January slump, which was a relief for everybody. During one five-game stretch, including a phenomenal 41-point, 19-rebound performance in a win over Philadelphia at the Forum, he totaled 173 points. With the Big Fella back on top of his game, we closed out February with seven straight wins.

March was another story. We lost three straight on the road and split a pair at home. Our defense became sluggish and our rebounding turned soft. The morning after a loss to Chicago, Riley held another team meeting to fire up our engines.

Unlike the scorcher a month earlier, Riley, more upset and disappointed than mad, focused on basketball issues, not moral ones. He went through every player and told him what he was doing wrong or wasn't doing at all. He was hard on a couple of the boys. One thing about Riley: he doesn't pull any punches.

"Magic," he said to me, "you've got to accept challenges on defense. You've got to say to yourself, 'I'm going to shut this man down,' and do it. In New York the other night, you gave Campy Russell that twenty-five-footer. Instead of playing up, you gave him room. Your hands were down by your side. You didn't even make an attempt. You might as well have said, 'Here, Campy,' and given him a free lane to the hoop."

The two players struggling the most were Coop and Norm. Norm, his knees sore from tendinitis, had a terrible February. Making the All-Star Game, he said, messed him up because he didn't get a chance to rest his knees. Riles got on Norm, but not like he lit into Coop.

"I don't know where you got the idea you're a star," Riley said to Mike, "because you're not. You're just a sub. It's about time you realized that. Last night you said you felt like a white dude. Well, I've got news for you, you're playing like one."

Riley was referring to a quote in the morning paper. Coop had blown a wide-open lay-up against the Bulls. I don't know why—whether he took off on the wrong foot or lost his balance—but he failed to get any lift on the jump, which for him was very unusual. As a result, he shot awkwardly and missed.

When a reporter asked him about the lay-up, Coop, believing the conversation to be off the record, had cracked, "It makes me feel like a white dude." The reporter, who was white, laughed. So did Coop. Another reporter overheard the comment while standing a few feet away and included it in his game story.

Coop cringed when he read the paper the next morning. Understanding immediately that many readers would interpret the remark as racist, he became extremely depressed. And that was before the team meeting. By the time Riley got through with him, he was shattered.

Mark Landsberger, another of Riley's main targets, was having a rough season. First he lost playing time to Kurt Rambis; along the way he lost more to Jim Brewer; and whatever time remained, he lost to McAdoo. A few weeks after Kupchak's injury, when the power-forward position was up for grabs, Riley gave Landsberger his first and only start. It came against Indiana, and it turned into a disaster.

Herb Williams, the Pacers' six-foot-ten-inch-rookie shot blocker, took Mark out of the game, blocking almost every shot he attempted.

By the time of Riley's March meeting, Mark wasn't playing much. When he did, he tried to do too much. Like shoot. He's an excellent rebounder, one of the best in the league, but he messes up when he grabs an offensive rebound and goes right back up with it instead of passing it out. Invariably he loses the ball on the shot; either it is stolen or blocked.

Riley, who had prepared extensive notes for the meeting, read them over before addressing Mark. There must have been a lot, because he was quiet for some time. Mark, knowing he was up, fidgeted.

"Mark," Riley said finally, "I don't mind you taking up an offensive rebound. You earned it; you deserved the shot. But don't make it tough. Don't fade away and shoot from the hip. You're inviting your man to block your shot. Think of a blocked shot as a message that the shot you just took was a bad one."

Riles even jumped on Kareem. He said, "I don't know where you were the whole New York trip. Guys were driving down the middle with impunity. It was like they were saying, 'Well, Kareem's standing in the lane, so I'll just go ahead and take it right to the hoop.'"

Riley's fairness is one of his strengths as a coach. He criticizes everybody who deserves it, not just a few. He hands out praise the same way. Me, Norm, Silk, Kareem, Coop— all of us. There are no favorites. And he will not be intimidated. Nothing upsets a player more than a coach who plays favorites. If you get blamed for doing something wrong and another player, who is equally at fault, doesn't, your immediate reaction is, "Hey, why should I have to take this?"

Riley eased up on rookies Mike McGee and Kevin McKenna, who hadn't been playing, and McAdoo, who hadn't recovered from the calf injury yet. At the end, he criticized himself.

"I've given you a lot of leeway because I respect you as professionals," he said. "You know what is expected of you and how to take care of yourselves. I believe you come ready to play, but I don't believe you are as ready as you must be. That, I believe, is my fault. It's up to me to better prepare you. I'd let you slide a little every time we'd win two or three in a row. Give you a day off to savor it a little longer. But this slide stuff is over. It's time to tune in to the work ethic if we're going to be ready for the playoffs."

Off days became history. Not only did we practice more frequently, but we practiced longer and harder. Nobody complained or dogged it. It was as though we had been waiting for Riley to take control. We worked relentlessly on defense, particularly on a half-court trap—constant two-man harassment of the ball handler—designed to force errors and accelerate the pace of the game. And give us more fast-break opportunities.

Coop's "white dude" comment created another controversy, another distraction. For once, I wasn't in the middle of it, but I felt badly for Coop. He didn't mean anything by it. It was an example of locker room talk that should have stayed there, not because the public doesn't have a right to know, but because the reader cannot possibly understand the spirit of the comment unless it is presented in the proper context. I don't know of a player in the league, white or black, who was offended by Coop's remark.

The reporter who overheard Coop understood. He didn't intend to stir the pot. Thinking it was a cute remark and believing it would be interpreted as such, he put it in his newspaper. However, in print it didn't look so cute. Readers' letters to the Los Angeles *Times* ripped Coop. Most accused him of being a "racist."

"You gotta watch it," I told Coop. "People don't understand."

He was really upset. "How could he put that in the paper?" He was almost in tears. "I wasn't even talking to him."

"You never know what they're going to write. That's why you have to be so careful with what you say, especially in the locker room. That's open territory."

"Man, I can't believe he put that in the paper. I'm no racist."

He worried me. Being extremely sensitive, Coop tends to dwell on a problem. I hoped it wouldn't stay with him to the point where it would interfere with his game.

"Just try to forget it," I said. "Try not to let it get you down."

I knew there wasn't anything anybody could say or do. What can you say? "Hey, Coop didn't mean that white dudes can't jump." People would say, "Oh. Then what did he mean?"

We speak a different language among ourselves, a language that's neither black nor white. It's basketball talk, a language that evolves from the interaction of a small group of people who share the same passion. In that isolated community, the color of a man's skin is as incidental as the color of a man's shorts. Teammates develop strong emotional ties that transcend race as well as religion, age, politics, and background. The game's the thing. A team divided, racially or otherwise, won't win.

The race issue really bothers me. I don't know why people keep saying the NBA is in trouble because 70 percent or more of its players are black. As long as the game is played the way fans like, what difference does it make if a player is white or black? To me, basketball is an art form that provides the artist with a means of satisfying his creative drive. The court is the canvas; the ball, the brush. When I go see a band, I don't care what color the musicians are. If it plays music I like, I'm going.

Coop worried that fans wouldn't love him anymore. He's enjoyed a warm relationship with the Forum fans since rocketing out of obscurity in 1979. They chant "Cooooop! Cooooop!" whenever he enters the game and go wild over his personalized high-wire Coop-a-loop dunks.

"Just play right through it," I advised. "If they boo, pretend they're saying 'Coop.' As soon as you dunk one for them, you'll be Mr. Excitement again."

I was speaking from experience—recent experience. Coop drew a few boos at the start of the next home game but won the fans back before the night was over.

Riley, true to his word, worked us hard daily, and we responded by ripping off five straight wins, including three on the road. Through all our ups and downs, especially the downs, I always found reassurance in our road record. We played well on the road, which meant we had the heart to play tough when it counted. I knew we'd be ready for the playoffs.

However, just as we appeared ready to roll, we stumbled backwards, losing to lowly Dallas by two points on a three-point jump shot by Mark Aguirre at the buzzer. It was at home, too. Riley was very upset.

"The Sonics are laughing at us right now!" he raged while wearing out the tiles in the locker room. "I can't deal with this 'can't-get-up-for-the-Mavericks' crap. How tough is it to get up for a game when you're in the middle of a division race?"

The Sonics probably did have a good laugh. They were making a move on our Pacific Division lead and had pulled to within two games, thanks to our defeat by Dallas. Riley was right to be mad. But whether Riley could deal with it or not, after winning five straight, we were unable to get ourselves up for the Mavericks. As players, we weren't happy, either. We messed up and blew a beautiful opportunity to put some distance between ourselves and Seattle. I knew I messed up. I had fifteen rebounds and fourteen assists but never got an offensive flow going. For the night, I took only four shots.

Riley, fearful that the Dallas loss might begin a trend, called another team meeting the day of the next game in San Antonio. Before doing so, he asked to meet with me privately in his room. We had just returned from shoot-around. Having no idea what was on his mind, I became apprehensive. I hoped I hadn't done or said anything wrong. Then I got scared, thinking there might be another blowup in the L.A. papers.

"Magic," Riley said when we had settled into the living room of his hotel suite, "I want your help."

Whew! Help? I'd give him all he wanted. On the outside I played it cool. I nodded while helping myself to an apple from the courtesy fruit basket on the coffee table.

"After the Chicago game," he continued, "we set specific standards. We were going to rebound better, pick up the pace of games, pick up our defensive assignments higher, run harder, everything. As a team, we pledged a total commitment to winning. With the exception of the Dallas game, we've played better, but I don't think we've met those standards."

I sat quietly and listened.

"The only way I'm ever going to enforce those standards is by having somebody out there willing to be totally and fully supportive. Now, I know how much winning means to you. And I know how badly you want this championship. For us to do it, this is what it's going to take. You, Magic, have to toe the line more than anybody. You have to set the example in practice. You have to be the one who pushes it and pushes it. Relentlessly."

He paused to light a cigarette. He took a deep drag, then exhaled. I watched him through the cloud of smoke; he was very intent. I knew how much winning meant to him, too.

"We only have a month left to get it together," he said. "I want to know if you're going to be with me."

I nodded absentmindedly, still listening.

"Will you take the responsibility? It's out there to be had—the real leadership of the team. I'm kind of amazed it's still there. Either nobody wants it, I guess, or it's too hot to handle. I'm not asking you to be the verbal leader. That would be difficult, if not impossible, with this group. I'm asking you to be the leader in spirit, the one who leads by example."

He looked at me, waiting for a response. He was through. "I know exactly where you're coming from," I said. "I'm with you."

Before playing the Spurs that night, Riley held what he called a "standards and procedures" meeting. He read a list of the standards that the team had set but failed to live up to.

"These are your standards," he said. "If you don't meet them on an individual basis, you come out of the game. It's that simple."

"You know, Riles," said Norm, "the only way for us to be aggressive—and win—is to put a lot of pressure on people full court. It's up to you to get us to do that."

"Why is it up to him?" asked Coop. "Why can't we just go out and do it on our own?"

Riley loved it. "Good point, Michael," he said. He laughed and turned to Norm. "What am I going to do? Flog you?"

It was an upbeat meeting. While everybody agreed that we hadn't lived up to our standards, we felt confident we would reach that level and be ready to roll right into the playoffs.

Then we went out and lost to the Spurs. I don't know why, but for some strange reason we always seemed to lose after one of Riley's meetings—I hoped we wouldn't have any more. But it didn't really matter. McAdoo was back. And, right after that loss to the Spurs, it was winning time.

We steamrolled over teams the last month of the regular season, stinging with the half-court trap and then trampling them with the fast break. We hummed like a finely-tuned Rolls-Royce. When we were right, which was most of the time, we left teams in our dust. We scored a season-high 153 points against Denver one night, 143 against San Diego, and 129 against Portland. We won 10 of our last 12

games, including the last three—scoring 128 points against
Utah, 125 against Golden State, and 120 at Phoenix.

We clinched the Pacific Division title in appropriate fashion—with a win over Seattle a week before the end of the
regular season. We finished 5 games in front, with a 57–25
record, and gladly accepted a bye through the first round of
the playoffs. We wanted nothing to do with the best-of-
three mini-series. The memory of losing to Houston was still
vivid.

Riley gave us the first two days off as we began our wait
for the winner of the Phoenix-Denver series. He told us to
go home and relax, to forget about basketball. Relaxing was
easy; forgetting about basketball was not. I was anxious to
begin. I felt confident about the team. And, despite the
rough times, I felt satisfied with my own season. I had led
the league in steals, finished second in assists, led the Lakers
in rebounding, and had the best field-goal percentage
among guards in the league. I also joined Oscar Robertson
and Wilt Chamberlain as one of only three players in NBA
history to get 700 or more rebounds and 700 or more assists
in the same season. Oscar did it three times, Wilt once. I'm
not sure exactly what the stat means, but I'll gladly join that
kind of company anyday.

I was also excited about being the president and majority
owner of an AM radio station in Evergreen, Colorado, a
suburb of Denver. The FCC had approved the purchase in
February. Since then, I'd gotten involved with the station as
much as time allowed. I worked with my consultants, Don
Wiskes and Jack Higgins; my attorneys, George and Harold
Andrews; my personal banker, Bob (Cash) McCall of the
First National Bank of Chicago; and the minority owners,
who include Tuck, Isiah Thomas, Mark Aguirre, and Herb
Williams. Along with them, I expanded the programming to
twenty-four hours and decided to retain the "oldies" musi-
cal format for the time being. This investment, perhaps
even more than those I have in real estate, oil, and gas, is
important to me because I still hope to make a career of

telecommunications—behind the camera, not in front of it—after basketball.

In the meantime, there was plenty of basketball left—the playoffs. Despite Riley's suggestion, I couldn't keep my mind off the game. The possibility of being champions again was right there, waiting for us; all we had to do was reach out and take it.

Even though the layoff could conceivably interrupt our momentum, having it was beautiful. Because we'd been running so hard, so much, and so well, it gave us a pause to recharge our batteries. Norm, with those sore knees, probably appreciated it more than anybody. This was no time, I had learned, to be running around town. Days off were too valuable to waste. I spent most of those two days flat on my back in bed. I slept, ate, and watched television. I got lucky and caught reruns of the old Sherlock Holmes movies. I've seen them all dozens of times, but I still love them.

We were sharp when practice resumed. Riley had toyed with the idea of scrimmaging San Antonio—which also drew a first-round bye, as the Midwest Division winner—at a neutral site equidistant between the two cities for a day or two during the break. He thought the competition would be good for us. But I was glad the plan fell through, and so was everybody else. That was the last thing we needed. We already knew how to tune up the fast break and set the half-court trap. Also, with the exception of Kurt Rambis, our top seven players all had playoff experience and knew what to expect: greater intensity, strength, endurance, and concentration. You have to play your best every game, every minute. The playoffs are for the money.

Riley put us through grueling practices to prepare us for both Phoenix and Denver. I'm sure we knew their offenses as well as they did. He gave videotapes of opposing players to each of the starters and key reserves. Studying them was our homework. I paid particular attention to the tape of Dennis Johnson of Phoenix. He is tough. Strong. He's dangerous, because he's the type of player who rises to the occasion. I knew he liked to post-up, so I studied his post-up moves on tape for hours. I'd try to keep him in the low twenties if I had to guard him. I couldn't let him score thirty or more.

The regular season ended on a Sunday, and we hoped to begin the Western Conference semifinals the following Sunday. One week's rest would have been perfect. But it didn't happen that way. We had to wait two more days because it took Phoenix three games to eliminate Denver.

We sprinted out of the gate in the first game against Phoenix and opened a 10-point lead after the first nine minutes. We never looked back and went on to win by 19. In Game 2 the next night, also at the Forum, we had the same result: a 19-point win. The Suns, unable to match our speed and quickness, were helpless against our trap and fast break. D.J. was all they had. He scored 20 and 27 the first two games.

Riley's decision to guard Walter Davis with Norm, instead of Coop, Silk, or me, was smart. Norm's superior quickness, Riley figured, would be more vital to containing Davis's explosive offense than height.

Davis, a former All-Pro forward who'd been shifted to guard the year before, had had a miserable season. He broke an elbow during a preseason game and missed the first third of the regular season. He wasn't the same when he rejoined the Suns and ultimately lost his starting job to Kyle Macy. But he had had a great series against Denver and had seemed as tough as ever. We expected to see a lot of him as the Suns' sixth man, and we did.

But Norm took him out. Even though Walter had a four- or five-inch height advantage, he didn't use it. I don't think he knew how. He always relied on quickness and speed to devastate the big guards and small forwards who usually guarded him. He isn't a post-up player. His game is lateral, meaning he makes his moves from side to side. Norm, being quicker, easily matched Davis's lateral moves.

In contrast, Norm would have been overmatched against D.J., who, though shorter than Walter, is still a few inches taller than Norm. D.J., like myself, plays a vertical game, meaning he is constantly moving to the hoop. It's up and down, from one hoop to the other. Since it is more of a power game, an advantage in height or weight is exposed at every opportunity.

Right at the end of the first half of the second game, I got a little scare. Actually, at the time, it was a big scare. While standing at the Suns' free-throw line, watching Dennis Johnson's half-court throw at the buzzer—pow!—I got hit on the side of the left knee by Phoenix's Larry Nance. While it was obviously an accident, his boxing me out for the rebound served no purpose considering the buzzer was just about to sound. My knee just gave out, like it had nothing in it. I collapsed to the floor in pain, and I mean pain. It was brutal. My first thought was, Oh, no, not again. Another knee injury would have blown me away.

Jack Curran ran out and eventually helped me to my feet. He led me to the training room, where I was examined by Dr. Kerlan. By then the sharp pain had subsided. Kerlan said it was just a bruise. He told me not to worry.

"Can I play the second half, Doc?" I asked.

He looked at me incredulously. "You'd better."

Just then the telephone rang. Dr. Kerlan answered.

"Magic," he said, turning around, "it's Dr. Tucker calling from Lansing. He wants to know if you're all right. You want to talk to him?"

"No," I said. "Just tell him it's cool."

Kerlan nodded and put the receiver to his ear. "It's cool," he said.

While listening to Chick Hearn's live broadcast, Tuck had gotten the impression that I was either dead or near death. I guess it looked that way from Chick's broadcast booth halfway up the stands.

Although the next two games were scheduled for Phoenix, there wasn't a great deal of suspense remaining in the series. At least, there wasn't any in my mind. Nor did I think there remained any in the minds of the Suns. They were beaten. You could read it in their comments.

"I think they're running better now than at any time I've seen them in the last five years," said John MacLeod, the Phoenix coach. "They got their running game going in early December and haven't stopped since."

"Their switching defense is driving the coaches crazy," said center Rich Kelley. "And us crazy."

By this time we were as tight as that quivering fist Riley had shown us during that team meeting early in February. Winning was the bottom line. Individual egos were subordinated to team ego. Each person understood his role within the team concept and knew we'd win if individual territory was covered. And, if a player wasn't doing his job, another player would tell him to get his butt moving.

It was: "Magic, get up on your man. Don't let him have that shot."

Or: "Kareem, close down the middle. We're counting on you, Big Fella."

Or: "Kurt, box that dude off the boards."

Or: "Mac, hang on to that pass. Concentrate."

Or: "Silk, don't release so early. Stay back on the defensive end a few seconds longer."

Nor did everybody go his separate ways on the road anymore. We ate together frequently. Sometimes as many as eight or nine of us would hit the movies, and we played cards—whist or tonk—for a few dollars to make it interesting.

I don't know how to accept losing. It doesn't matter what it is—basketball, cards, craps. Nor do the stakes matter, big or small. I always believe I'll win. If I lose, I don't give up. I want to go again, and again, and again, until I do win.

I was in tough company in Phoenix. Cards, I mean, not basketball. I played tonk with Norm, Dr. Kerlan, and Dr. Steve Lombardo, Dr. Kerlan's associate. Dr. Kerlan knows about winning, too. He's a good cardplayer, as are Norm and Dr. Lombardo. While we played a serious game, we also played to have fun. We laughed and screamed the whole time. At least Norm and I did. Dr. Kerlan and Dr. Lombardo, being more reserved types, were less vocal. But in their quiet way, they had just as much fun.

"Doc," Norm said to Kerlan, "bring out that roll."

"I'll bring it out, but all you'll ever do is look," Kerlan said. He carried a large roll of bills.

"I take rolls," I told him.

"Not this one you won't."

"That's Doc's endless knot," said Norm.

"You're right," said Kerlan. "And do you know why it's endless? Because I never lose."

"Until today, Doc," I said.

The card games continued throughout our stay. Sitting next to each other, Norm and I were big winners the first day. Dr. Kerlan separated us the second day.

"Just in case," he said.

"Just in case of what?" asked Norm.

"The Doc can't handle losing," I told Norm.

"No," Dr. Kerlan said, "that isn't it. I can handle losing if I lose fair and square."

"Ohhhh!" Norm and I howled. "The Doc is accusing us of cheating."

We weren't cheating, but the new seating arrangement worked for both doctors. They made their comebacks, and by the time we left everybody was just about even.

If the Suns weren't finished *before* the third game, they were *five minutes into it*. After Kareem made the first basket of the game, the Suns scored ten straight points. Then we got serious. We outscored them 12–2 over the next two minutes to erase any hopes they might have had. We ran them out in the third quarter, our quarter. When we're playing well, we always come out of halftime smoking.

In the fourth game, we fully concentrated on winning. We wanted the sweep. As far as we were concerned, this was the seventh and deciding game. The Suns felt the same way. They wanted to avoid the embarrassment of being swept. They played their hearts out, but we just wouldn't let them have the game.

Then we had a week off while San Antonio's series dragged on. Norm welcomed it because it gave him another opportunity to rest his knees. But this layoff worried some of the rest of us. We were rolling so well, and we hoped nothing would break that spell. But of course there was no sense in worrying, because there was nothing we could do about it.

San Antonio won its series, and once we knew the Spurs would be our next opponent, we had something worth worrying about—George Gervin and Mike Mitchell, their one-two offensive punch. Either one can hit you for 40 and not leave a scratch. We wanted to run, as usual, and hopefully to keep those two from killing us. This afternoon, Mother's Day, they got their points—Ice had 34 and Mitchell 25—but they didn't kill us.

Later, though, I thought about killing Tuck. I couldn't believe he tricked me like that. And he knows how much I hate surprises. But how can I stay mad when I see my mother's smile? Tuck knows that, too.

We stopped at the supermarket on the way home from the Forum. Mom plans to stay a few days and wanted to load up on groceries. She likes cooking for me, which will be great.

She says she wants to see the sights while she's out here: Universal Studios, the beaches, Hollywood, movie stars' homes. She also wants to visit a few flea markets—she loves those—and shop on Rodeo Drive in Beverly Hills. I better find somebody to take her around because I won't have the time. I also better go to the bank first thing tomorrow and withdraw some cash. She usually does more looking than buying, and I hope the pattern holds true on Rodeo Drive. Otherwise, we better win the NBA championship for the money as well as the pride.

11

Showtime

Right at the start of my rookie season in 1979–80, pro basketball was what I'd dreamed it would be. I knew I'd love the NBA. It was where I belonged, my reward for thousands of hours of practice and all those nights of dreams.

San Diego—a dramatic win at the buzzer—was an appropriate beginning to my professional career, and it launched me on a four-day high while waiting for our home opener against Chicago. The Lakers' publicity department pumped up the event, bringing in real magicians to entertain customers before the game, Glen Campbell to sing the national anthem, and the University of Southern California's Marching Band and Song Girls to perform during breaks. We drew a near-sellout crowd, which everybody said was great in view of the mid-October sports logjam: the World Series, the pro-football Rams, college football, and ice hockey. I was disappointed—I wanted the Forum jammed. But, anyway, we turned on those fans who were there and got the building rocking with a few fast breaks and a win.

After two games, I felt great. I had 45 points, 17 rebounds, 12 assists—and two wins. What an emotional high. I didn't think I'd ever come down.

Wrong. I crash-landed in Seattle the next night while going for a rebound. I hooked legs with Jack Sikma of the SuperSonics and twisted my right knee. I immediately crumpled, the pain unbearable. Jack Curran wrapped my knee in ice and helped me off the floor. The Seattle team doctor examined me in the training room. He looked at my knee, felt it, asked where it hurt, and broke the bad news. He told me I had a partially torn ligament and would be out from six to eight weeks—if all went well.

Six to eight weeks!

I almost cried. It couldn't be. Just like that—pow!—my year was all but over. I couldn't talk. Or think. The pain in my knee was nothing compared with the pain in my heart. After the game, the guys tried to cheer me up, which helped some but not enough to alleviate the overwhelming sense of injustice I felt. To have my dream suddenly snatched away wasn't fair. Moreover, the injury was a frightening one. A torn knee ligament can ruin a basketball player.

Curran wrapped the knee tightly in an adhesive bandage and put me on crutches.

"Do I have to use these?" I asked.

"Yes," he said. "We're going to see Dr. Kerlan first thing in the morning. Stay in bed and keep the wrap on. If you have to get up, use the crutches. Don't go hopping around. We've got an early flight, so I'll call you when it's time to get up."

Dr. Buss leased a private jet to get me to Los Angeles as quickly as possible. The earliest departure he could arrange was 6:45 the next morning. That night I wished he could have arranged one right after the game. My hotel room was a lonely place to be. I kept thinking my season was over. It never occurred to me the doctor might be wrong.

I spent most of the sleepless night on the telephone talking to my father and Tuck. They were down, too. All they could say was hang in there and work hard. "Being young is a plus," said Tuck. "You'll heal faster." To top it all off, my parents had planned to visit L.A. to watch me play pro ball for the first time. They had been looking forward to it; so had I.

"No sense you coming now," I told my dad.

"We're coming," he said.

"You won't see me play."

"It doesn't matter."

I was glad they were coming; I needed their support. I could have used it that night.

Curran put me together in the morning. I don't think I said a word the entire flight. I was too tired and depressed. From the L.A. airport, we went straight to Dr. Kerlan's office. I limped in on crutches.

"What did you do, Magic?" Dr. Kerlan asked.

"I don't know." I closed my eyes as I lay down on the examination table.

About an hour later, the examination completed, I said to Dr. Kerlan, "Well, what is it?"

Kerlan began chuckling as he massaged my knee. I opened my eyes to see him smiling.

"What's so funny?"

"We're going to have to amputate above the knee," he said. He chuckled again.

"What're you talking about?"

"There's nothing wrong with you. Your knee is sprained, that's all."

"That's all?"

"That's all." He chuckled some more.

"How long will I be out?"

"A week. Maybe ten days."

"Whoa!" I screamed. "You're not kidding me, are you Doc?"

"No, I'm not kidding you."

"Whoa!" I screamed again. I couldn't believe it. Maybe, I thought, there was somebody up there looking over me after all.

Down here, my teammates were looking me over—very carefully. They knew I could play, but that wasn't enough. More important was being able to play with them and win. NCAA champion, NCAA Tournament MVP, All-American, No. 1 draft pick, the nickname, commercials and endorsements, the smile, the reams of publicity. None of that mattered. I had to prove myself to them, and if anything the star treatment made my job more difficult. It was like "Magic, huh? Okay, show us some magic."

So I just went out and gave them what I had. I expected some coolness and got it. But it wasn't bad. Kareem, for example, was great. He went his own way and never tried to inhibit me. At times he'd get wrapped up in the enthusiasm; other times he wouldn't. That was fine with me, because I had no desire to push anything on him, or anybody else. Kareem, being so secure in his own position, was content to let me be.

Norm felt my presence the most. Just as I felt his. I don't think any two people, regardless of their business or the length of their relationship, can enter into a partnership expecting it to click from the start. As a result, Norm and I had our share of problems while trying to work the technical bugs out of our backcourt combination. He had no way of knowing, for example, that I could come off the boards with a rebound and immediately go into the fast break. When Norm would cut into the middle for the outlet pass, as he was taught, I'd wave him off, telling him to fill the lane, where he'd get the open jump shot. Neither one of us had ever played before with a guard who could handle the ball and direct the fast break. Adjustments were necessary, and making them took time. In the end, it was time well spent.

We were always running into each other those first few months. We'd arrive at the same place at the same time, then—whoa!—one would have to move out. It frustrated Norm, I think, because he was a Laker first. Which I understood. But it was up to him to understand that I was a Laker, too. We talked about our roles and responsibilities for hours at a time and eventually learned the other's game. Once we did, we reacted instinctively and played beautifully together. Basically, we shared the ball. When he had it, I got out and ran; when I had it, he ran. By the end of the season, we were really clicking. If he did this, I did that—bam bam— everything automatic. We were reading each other so well and so accurately that words no longer were needed to communicate. One look was all it took. I didn't think there was a backcourt in the league that could match us.

Add Michael Cooper, my training-camp partner who barely escaped the final preseason cut, to the equation, and we had the Three Musketeers—the baddest trio of guards in basketball. Indirectly I gave Coop his big chance. It came during those three games I missed with the sprained knee. In the first game, Coach Jack McKinney started Ron Boone, a veteran who was approaching the end of a long and productive career. For the second game, Coach McKinney switched to Coop. Coop scored nineteen points in his first NBA start, and three days later McKinney traded Boone to Utah for Marty Byrnes.

Ten days after that, while on his way to play tennis with Paul Westhead, McKinney fell off a bicycle and suffered serious head injuries. I didn't know how bad the injuries were at first. Nobody seemed to. The front office was being very tight-lipped about it. Westhead, who'd stayed in the background under McKinney, took over, and a few weeks later he officially became interim head coach. He named Pat Riley as his assistant coach.

Days, games, ups and downs come and go so quickly that you lose perspective of the real world outside the arenas. The full impact of McKinney's injuries didn't strike me until months later. In the beginning, I'd assumed he'd be back soon. Then I went on to more immediate concerns, like the next game and the players I'd have to face.

I learned quickly that soft touches were rare. The amount of talent in the NBA is amazing. George Gervin? He's impossible to stop. You try to control him and just hope he doesn't dominate the game. That's all you can do. He's too much, too slippery. George is so tough because *he* doesn't know what he's going to do next. If he doesn't, how can the defender know? He's the premier scorer in the game.

Some of the other top guards are Norm, Dennis Johnson, Gus Williams, World Free, and Michael Ray Richardson in the West. In the East you have Isiah Thomas, Reggie Theus, Andrew Toney, Maurice Cheeks, and Otis Birdsong. I think John Long can become a good guard with a little work. Sidney Moncrief is super tough because he never lets up. If you don't watch out, he'll be over the rim dunking on you in an instant. And, of course, Nate Archibald. Because he controls the flow of the game, Boston wouldn't be nearly as good without him. He scores. He's smart. He knows how to get into the seams to make something happen. That's the key to becoming a good guard—reading the seams. Tiny must have been a terror before tearing up his Achilles tendon.

Another great guard—when he's right—is David Thompson. He's an incredible athlete. Runs, jumps. He's explosive and quick. He'll shoot the jumper right in your eye. He doesn't care—he knows you can't block it. Like George, David, when he's in a groove, is unstoppable.

Among the centers, Kareem is king of the hill. I don't care how old he is. Moses Malone is the toughest rebounder in the league. Nobody comes close. Robert Parish is another excellent center. So are Artis Gilmore and Jack Sikma. But who would you choose to play the pivot for you in a money game? I'd choose the Big Fella. He knows how to get the job done.

Julius Erving and Larry Bird are the best forwards. What makes the Doc great is his leaping ability. The man can soar. While he doesn't go as high as some guys—like Michael Cooper, for example—he has the uncanny ability to hang and move while airborne. That's how he makes those incredible shots. You never know where it's coming from— left-handed, right-handed, finger roll, reverse, slam, off the board. He makes some amazing moves around the hoop; I swear he sometimes changes direction in midair. Physics professors should watch him play. I'd like to hear how they explain his moves.

As good as Doc is, I think Larry is better. Larry is so smart he doesn't have to score to hurt you. He's always zipping in and out, scoring, rebounding, passing, making the steal, bringing the ball upcourt. He can dominate a game without scoring a point. He'll be one of the all-time greats before he's through.

Not only did I have to contend with guys like that my first season, I also had to contend with a totally new life-style. You talk about fast—life in the NBA is a blur. It's night after night, city after city. On the road you go from airplane to bus to hotel room to coffee shop to arena and back again. Three games in three nights in three cities is not uncommon. It is a brutal test of endurance.

A player goes through three steps of consciousness on the road. First, he is excited by the life. New cities, first-class plane tickets and accommodations, good food, new faces, new things to do, and enough pocket change to do it with. Second, it overwhelms him. He stops going out because he's too tired. When he gets up in the morning, he has no idea where he is. Third, it bores him. The road becomes room service and television. When he wakes up in the morning, he no longer cares where he is. He's learned it doesn't matter. Once he drags himself out of bed, packs his bag, and

makes the bus on time, he hands over control of his life to
the team. He is herded to the next destination along with
everybody else.

Then there are the ladies who try to break the monotony
of a player's life on the road by donating their services.

"Hello, Magic" a sweet voice will purr on the telephone.

Silence. If I don't recognize the voice, sometimes I won't
reply. But the silence doesn't last long.

"Can I come up and satisfy you?" the voice purrs on.

I just say, "Not now, baby. I have to get my sleep for the
game tonight."

The big question she eventually asks is, "What's your
room number?"

"Sorry," I'll say, "it's been fun. 'Bye."

Every now and then they find out the room number and
knock on the door. I've learned to check out the visitor
through the peephole before answering. You have to be
careful, because it's all over once they know you're in
there.

There are some funny ones out there. I don't know how
many times I've been pinched on the butt. It's unbelievable. While most are harmless, others aren't.

"Every move you make, I'm right behind you." That's
what one woman whispered into my ear as I signed autographs for a group of kids outside the Forum one night. She
smiled seductively as I turned to face her.

"Are you serious?" I asked.

She nodded.

"You going to follow me forever?" I'd play her game if
that's what she wanted.

"Yes," she hissed.

I took a good look into her eyes and decided I'd rather
not play her game after all. This was a strange one. In the
meantime, I continued signing autographs.

"Well," I said, trying to be casual so as not to alarm the
kids, "I don't think this is a good time. I'm on my way to
meet someone."

"It doesn't matter where you go," she said. "Every move you make, I'm right behind you."

As I slowly moved through the crowd, still signing, I'd turn around every now and then to see where she was. Every time she'd be right there, as she'd said she would, smiling. Deciding she might be too far-out, I picked up my pace. I cut off the autographs and hurried to my car. As I pulled out of the Forum parking lot, I looked into the rearview mirror. Unbelievable. She was in the passenger's seat of the car behind me—another girl was driving. I headed for the San Diego Freeway, where I hit the accelerator on the open road and lost her for the night and, hopefully, for good. When the coast was clear, I doubled back and drove home.

Although this incident was unusual and somewhat bizarre, it nonetheless was an example of the price the celebrity-athlete must pay. My attorneys and advisers, George and Harold Andrews, warned me about that before the start of the season.

"You have to pay a price when you make commercials and endorse products and concepts," George told me during one meeting. "You have to make yourself more accessible to the public, which will interfere with your private life. I know you like people and draw energy from them, but potentially the demands are staggering. Some guys who have the opportunities you have turn them down. They don't want the spotlight. To them, the price is too steep. They'd rather have privacy."

Having already had a taste of celebrity life and its demands, I decided to go for it. Before doing so, we established a set of guidelines. First, it had to be a quality product, one that I liked and enjoyed using. I couldn't go up there and say "Try this" when I had no intention of trying it myself. It also had to be consistent with my personality and what I represented as an individual.

The same guidelines applied to promotions. Before the

1980 presidential election, a White House staff member contacted Harold to inquire if I would be interested in promoting the Selective Service. I was flattered, but I wasn't interested. It would have been hypocritical of me—being six foot nine and too tall for the draft—to tell kids to join the Army.

Furthermore, we tried to be selective to avoid overexposure. As George likes to say, "You're not a box of cereal." This plan served several purposes: it gave those I did business with a degree of exclusivity; it allowed me some time and privacy to grow as an individual; and, for the most part, it precluded interference with basketball, which besides making my outside activities possible, was the only thing that counted.

I quickly learned everybody wants a piece of the action. When you're hot, hands holding business cards reach out from every direction.

"Magic, I'm opening a sporting goods store, and with your name...."

"Magic, I have this great idea for a poster. You're spinning a basketball on your finger and—get this, you'll love it—you're only wearing a jock strap. It'll be the hottest-selling poster in the country...."

"Magic, if you're into health foods...."

"Magic, would you like to invest in my restaurant?..."

"Magic, how about a clothing store?..."

Usually, they'd want me to put up all the capital for a percentage of the business. I'd listen once in a while—a few would sound interesting—and refer them to George or Harold.

"Explain it to my attorneys," I'd say. I'd hand over the Andrews & Andrews business card. "Then, they'll get back to me and we'll see."

While I sometimes hide out to avoid the constant interview and personal-appearance requests, I always make time for kids. I love kids. To me, there isn't a sweeter sound in the world than a child's laughter. We relate well to each other—they know I'm not tricking them when I tell them how it is. Kids can usually detect insincerity.

"Why don't you do three-sixty dunks like David Thompson?" a boy asked me at a basketball camp one day.

"That's not my game," I said.

"Then he's better."

"How many points do you get for a three-sixty dunk?" I asked.

"Two."

"How many points do you get for a little jumper in the lane?"

"Two."

"Then what's the difference?"

"The three-sixty is more exciting."

"Winning is even more."

Kids learn about winning early, from playing games in school, playgrounds, and the streets. They love the immediate sensation of victory, and, in a few cases, the lingering joy of being king of the hill. In the process, they also learn about losing, which all too often they see too much around them. So, when somebody talks to them about winning— what it means and what it takes—they listen. They like being in the company of somebody they perceive as a winner.

Which is why I always try to sign autographs. Each one is important to the boy or girl requesting it, even though it often winds up in the trash. The thought, which endures, is more meaningful than the slip of paper. The kid remembers the moment when so-and-so gave him an autograph, just as he remembers the moment so-and-so turned him down. Unfortunately, even the most cooperative athlete sometimes has to say no. There are those, however, who aren't cooperative at all, and I think it hurts them in the long run. When I know I can't stay and sign autographs for everybody, I establish a cut-off point. "Five more and that's it," I'll say, "because I have to go." I sign many more than that, but eventually my announcement brings the signing session to an end, usually without any problems. But not always.

After a softball game in upstate Michigan one hot and humid summer day, I signed for about thirty minutes. Finally, I couldn't take the heat any longer. It was brutal. I was amazed that the kids stayed. So, after setting my cut-off and signing the last one, I started walking off. One disappointed little girl ran into her mother's arms. "He won't sign my autograph," she cried. Oh, that hurt. The mother understood, and she tried to explain to her daughter why I hadn't given her my autograph. It didn't help. The girl wailed away. I couldn't leave like that. I kneeled beside her and wiped away her tears. I took her book, signed it, and gave it back.

"You okay?" I asked.

She nodded and, through the tears still flooding her eyes, smiled. "Thank you, Magic," she said. She was a pretty little girl.

I might have made her day and her mother's as well, but I'll bet she never knew how much she had done for mine.

The toughest burden of all for an NBA rookie is the killer schedule. Eighty-two regular-season games. Add at least seven in the preseason, and as many as twenty in the playoffs, and you have a season nearly four times as large as the one in college.

By mid-season of my rookie year I was burned out—both mentally and physically. My legs felt like lead. Then, in mid-January, I pulled a hamstring muscle. In retrospect, that might have been the best thing that happened to me because I got some time off. It really upset me at the time, though, because it spoiled my homecoming. The injury occurred right before the Detroit game—our only visit of the season there. I probably shouldn't have played, but I had to. A record crowd—more than 28,000—turned out for my return to Michigan. It might not have been much, but I gave them what I could. After that I was able to sit out some games and rest.

The Lakers came together as a team the second half of the season. From the last day of January until the end of the regular season, we won twenty-three games and lost only five. We had winning streaks of seven games in February, five in mid-March, and five to close out the season at the end of March.

Westhead, who'd had conflicts with forwards Spencer Haywood and Jim Chones, settled on Chones as the starting power forward. Haywood, the starter at the beginning of the year, couldn't accept a bench role. It put his ego out of joint. He had been a major star earlier in his career—an Olympic gold medalist in 1968, first-team All-League in the old American Basketball Association at the age of twenty, then first- or second-team NBA All-League four straight seasons. By the 1979–80 season, however, his skills showed signs of wear and tear.

"You don't understand," he'd always say, "I need to play."

Spencer had a macho thing going, always talking about his manliness and how we needed him to "put some authority on the floor." He wasn't the easiest person to get along with. Whenever I'd make a suggestion, he'd rebuke me. He'd say, "I've been in the league eleven years. You can't tell me nothing." That rap got old quickly, so I stopped making suggestions.

He had a big blowup with Westhead after a Sunday-night game at the Forum. I first heard about it at the airport the next morning. It was all over the papers. Westhead had told reporters after the game that Spencer hadn't played because an allergy problem had kept him from practicing the day before. When Spencer heard this, he blew up and called Westhead a liar. He insisted he had practiced that day. Paul, unappreciative of being called a liar in print, called Spencer in the morning and told him to stay home, supposedly to see a doctor for treatment of the allergy. Sure enough, Spencer wasn't on board the flight that took us east for a two-game road trip.

On the surface, the issue was: What constitutes a practice? Spencer's brief participation in the light drills at the beginning of the workout did not satisfy Westhead's definition. But it did satisfy Spencer's, which was a looser interpretation. The root of the conflict was that Spencer's playing time had all but vanished because Westhead had been using forward Don Ford ahead of him. This was a severe infringement on Spencer's manliness. Playing behind Chones, an established pro, was one thing; playing behind Ford, a journeyman, was another. Dr. Buss got involved over the next few days and patched up the disagreement as soon as the team returned from the trip. After meeting with player and coach, he reinstated Haywood.

I don't know whether Dr. Buss's involvement had any bearing on it or not, but Spencer's playing time suddenly increased. And as it did, so did the quality of his play. Then, on the sidelines during a game at Milwaukee, Westhead jumped all over Chones because of his defense. Jimmy jumped right back and cursed Westhead. The next game, Haywood was a starter again. But Chones soon got the job back—permanently.

I recovered from my injury about the same time Chones recovered the starting power forward position. I had also gotten my wind back, and I began turning it out the rest of the way. So did the rest of the guys. The growing pains were gone. My teammates knew where I was coming from. More important, we were all headed for the same destination—the championship. I was still a rookie, but I wasn't under the microscope any longer. They pulled for me as I pulled for them, and, in one instance, they even stood by me.

That happened when Pat Riley, who was the assistant coach at the time, tore into me as I headed for the bench for a time-out during a tough game against the New Jersey

Nets. It was early February. At the time-out, the game appeared to be slipping away. On consecutive fast breaks moments earlier I'd taken the ball to the hoop instead of hitting Chones, who was open both times on the wing.

"Magic," said Riley, pulling me aside. "Hit Jimmy when he's open like that. He's busting his ass filling those lanes and deserves to get the ball."

It was a frustrating night for everybody, struggling the way we were against a team we should have been killing. I was tense. So was Riley.

"Damn," I said, throwing my arms down at my sides, "I can't do anything right." I took a seat between Kareem and Jimmy.

"Are they messing with you again?" Kareem asked.

I appreciated his concern and support. "No, it's all right. I just have to settle down."

"It's all right," Jimmy said, patting my knee. "Everything's cool."

Once my teammates accepted me, everybody had fun. Including the fans. L.A.'s passive fans? What passive fans? They were anything but. They went wild over the running game and the way we pulled for each other, hugging, slapping, pointing, mugging, and laughing. At my press conference the previous May, Chick Hearn had predicted attendance would increase by an average of 2,000. The actual figure was nearly 2,500. It was showtime.

We were a confident team entering the playoffs. We'd picked up power forward Mark Landsberger from Chicago in mid-February, and he firmed up our rebounding, which had been soft. We finished the regular season with a 60–22 record and won the Pacific Division title by four games over Seattle, the defending NBA champion.

"I don't see anybody beating us," Norm said before our first playoff series. I agreed, even though I hadn't experienced the playoffs yet. I had heard how games were more intense, more physical, and how much tougher it was to score. That didn't faze me.

We rolled over our first opponent, Phoenix, in five games. Next, we played Seattle. All season long we'd been saying the Sonics were the team to beat. We expected a long, tough series, and after the first game—a one-point loss at home—it suddenly looked like it might be tougher than we thought. That game was a heartbreaking defeat for us. Jack Sikma made the winning point on a free throw with 2 seconds to go. It had been a rebounding foul under *our* basket.

We won the second game and headed to Seattle needing a split of the next two games to regain the home-court advantage. Late in the second quarter of Game 3, Haywood, who'd just entered the game, posted up and waved for the ball. I'd seen him but decided to go the other way, where I thought we had a better opportunity. The game was tight—and important.

"Goddamnit," Spencer said to me on the way downcourt. "I got a good post-up. Give me the damned ball when I'm open."

He made me so mad I almost turned purple—I couldn't believe he was cussing me out. I had no idea where his head was. This was the furthest he'd ever been in the playoffs in his career and he'd let himself go. He was out of shape and mentally unprepared. That night, he looked like he was in a trance. I was surprised the coach even put him in the game.

A couple of minutes later we went into our "41" play for the final shot of the half, trailing by four points. The play was designed to spread us out on the court. I handled the ball at the point while everybody else set up along the baseline. As I drove the lane, Sikma jumped out at me, leaving Spencer wide open under the hoop. I put it right into Spencer's hands. The pass was soft, perfect. I stood there in shock as the ball bounced off his hands and out of bounds. Then he had the nerve to tell me I'd given it to him at the wrong time, because he hadn't had a chance to get his footing.

That did it. "I can't play with him," I said while walking

off court. I was just talking, but I didn't care who heard me. "He's too crazy. He wants its, and then he loses it."

We rallied the second half and won. Two days later we blew the Sonics away with an incredible rally. Behind by 21 points midway through the third period, we turned on the jets and won by five, giving us a sweep in Seattle and a 3–1 series lead. We finished them in Game 5 to enter the championship finals against the Philadelphia 76ers.

I was ready. We all were. With one exception—Haywood.

He was something. During the playoffs, Kareem's lady friend made elaborate plans for a surprise party to celebrate Kareem's thirty-third birthday. Keeping the surprise was a vital part of the planning, but it was difficult because of the large number of people invited.

The morning of the party Kareem was still in the dark. However, at practice, during the middle of the stretching exercises, Spencer called out, "Hey, Kareem. What time's your party tonight?" This party had been in the works for months. A couple of guys groaned in disbelief.

Then, two days before the finals, Spencer fell asleep in practice. First he dozed off while watching films of Philadelphia before practice. We died in the film room. Spencer actually snored. We laughed on the outside; inside we were upset. We knew he wasn't with us and was incapable of helping out if we needed him.

After staggering out of the film room, he began stretching on the gym floor with the rest of us. Everybody else was feeling great, talking and laughing as Jack Curran bellowed out one exercise after another. Spencer, meanwhile, was lying flat on his back—sleeping—a few feet outside our exercise circle.

Coop noticed him first. "Spencer," he said softly.

No response.

"Spencer." Softly again.

Spencer didn't move. Other players began noticing. So did Curran, the coaches, and a half dozen or so reporters who were watching from the sidelines.

Curran went over and tried to wake him. "Hey, Woody," he said sharply.

Spencer still did not budge. Curran then kneeled beside him and nudged gently. Still nothing. Finally, Curran grabbed him and shook him. Spencer snapped out of his sleep and, after taking a few seconds to gather himself, groggily left the practice floor.

Spencer had an explanation. He always had one.

"Because I've been lifting weights and running on my own, my body tightened during the night and I couldn't get any sleep," he said. "I was sick from exhaustion at practice. . . .

"I'm not getting enough playing time," he continued, "so I have to get into shape on my own. I know the team will need me in the Philadelphia series."

We won the first game of that series in L.A. Then, two days later, Haywood arrived ten minutes late for practice, which might have gone unnoticed had it not been for his earlier behavior. He should have stayed away, because practicing with him had become a waste of time. He was still pouting over a lack of playing time.

The curtain dropped on Spencer the next night, as Philadelphia evened the series at 1–1. He was a constant source of distraction during the game. He'd stand on the fringe of the time-out huddle, holding a towel around his neck, and bounce up and down to encourage fans who chanted for him. He also talked to the people behind the bench, saying, "I'm not part of this." He was right about that. To top it off, he got into an argument with Brad Holland over a tape cutter in the locker room.

Westhead had had enough. He suspended Haywood for the rest of the season for "activities disruptive toward the team." We'd all had enough. What was he doing? Trying to mess us up? This was his chance to be a champion, and he blew it.

We just went on without him. We split the two games in Philadelphia and returned to Los Angeles for Game 5 and

yet another compelling off-the-court story. Buss, reacting to
news that originated in Philadelphia, announced that Jack
McKinney would not return to coach the Lakers next
season.

In the locker room, we were wondering what in the
world was going on. We were trying to win a championship
and distractions kept popping up—first Spencer, then
McKinney. What next?

We found out the next night. Towards the end of the
third period, Kareem sprained his left ankle badly. He left
the floor and returned for the fourth period with the ankle
heavily wrapped. He turned in a courageous performance,
scoring 14 of his 40 points in that fourth period, including
the three points—on a dunk and free throw—that won the
game. Those would be his last points of the season. The
ankle was in such bad shape that the team doctors made
him stay in Los Angeles while we went to Philadelphia for
Game 6. The doctors hoped they could make the ankle fit
for a seventh game. We were up, three games to two,
needing one more for the title.

At the airport we learned we were going to Philadelphia
for the sixth game without him. I assumed Chones would
move to center, I'd play forward, and Coop would start at
guard. But before boarding the flight, Westhead said, "E.J.,
you're starting at center tomorrow night." He was smiling.
"That's fine with me," I said. I thought he was joking. On
the airplane, I took the seat Kareem usually sat in, the first
one on the left. As the guys boarded, I kept saying, "Don't
worry, the Big Fella's here." Everybody got a big laugh.

That night Jim, Coop, Norm, Silk, Mark, and I got together in one of the rooms. It wasn't planned. We were on the
same floor, and guys just started popping in.

"Do you believe nobody thinks we can win this game?" I
asked.

"We're going to run them out," Chones said.

We figured Jimmy, Mark, and I had to hit the boards
hard. Silk had to pick up the scoring slack not only for

Kareem but also for Norm, who had broken a finger on his left hand in Game 5. If it had been any other time of year, Norm would have sat out. Mainly, we knew we had to run—all game. We had to run after makes as well as misses. We knew we could not let up. We had to shock them.

At shoot-around, Westhead told me to run the plays in the pivot. Wow, I thought, he wasn't kidding. I felt great all day. I knew we were going to win. And I knew I was going to have a great game.

I called my father before taking my pregame nap. "Dad," I said, "go on back to high-school days. I'm going to turn back the clock tonight."

We were loose in the locker room before the game. The music was going and the conversation flowing.

"Philly better be ready for us," I said. "They're going to see the new Lakers."

We talked about the newspaper stories and radio and television broadcasts that day. Everybody was speculating about Kareem's availability for the seventh game.

"I've got news for them," I said. "There won't be a seventh game."

I jumped center against Caldwell Jones and ran a few plays in the post. But I played everywhere—center, forward, guard. As I'd told my dad, it was high school all over again. I turned it out.

We took the early lead and then survived Philly's first push. The Sixers caught us but couldn't go ahead. That was a good sign. A better sign was our rebounding. We controlled the boards, which allowed us to control the tempo. The 60–60 halftime score, being so high, was yet another good sign.

"We're right there!" everybody shouted as we entered the locker room. We pumped each other up, really got the adrenaline flowing. And we were entering the third period, which all year had been our best period. We were ready to blast off.

We scored the first 14 points of the second half. Philly

was stunned. The Spectrum crowd was silent. The 76ers, behind Julius Erving, made their final push midway through the fourth period. They cut our lead to 2 points four times before we put on a 10–2 spurt that gave us a 10-point lead with only 1:50 to go. We were the champs. Everybody had played a great game. I had 42 points, 15 rebounds, and 7 assists. Silk scored 37, including 25 in the second half. Norman couldn't shoot because of the broken finger but played a great floor game, passing off for 9 assists and making one of the biggest plays of the night. He stole a pass by Dr. J. and hit me for a basket that started our 10–2 rally. Chones had 11 points and 10 rebounds, Coop had 16 points, Landsberger had 10 boards. And Brad Holland, who hadn't played much all that year, came through when it counted to score 8 points in nine minutes of play.

The locker room afterwards was relatively quiet. Everybody was dead tired. But happy. We were the 1979–80 NBA champs. We looked at each other and said, "We did it."

Rick Barry, a CBS announcer and a former NBA great, said to me, "This is the quietest championship locker room I've ever been in."

"Hey," I said, "if you ran up and down the court the way we did for forty-eight minutes nonstop, you'd be kind of quiet, too."

I felt bad that Kareem wasn't there to celebrate the championship. He'd been through the whole season, it wasn't right that he had to miss the big game. But I was very happy.

On camera, Rick asked what I could possibly do for an encore.

I smiled and shrugged. "Win it again next year," I said. "Then win another and another and another. I never get tired of winning."

12

Bad Days

The last team to win back-to-back NBA championships was
Boston, in the playoffs of 1968 and 1969. I thought we had a
good chance to do it, too, because for the 1980–81 season,
the nucleus of our 1979–80 team, with the exception of
Spencer Haywood, was back. All we had to do was pick up
where we left off and keep the roll going. Our major adjustments had been made.

But I couldn't count on tearing cartilage in my left knee
one month into the season and missing forty-five games.
There was no way I could predict the turmoil and the new
adjustments my injury would create. Having never been
seriously injured, I could not imagine the ordeal I would
have to go through.

My problems began on a Tuesday night in Atlanta. Tom
Burleson, a gangling seven-foot-three-inch center for the

Atlanta Hawks, fell on top of me under the Hawks' basket and raked my left knee with the big iron bars protruding from his heavy-duty protective knee brace.

The Laker coaches had complained about Burleson's brace at the start of the game. The contraption looked dangerous. "He's going to tear somebody's leg open with that thing!" Paul Westhead shouted to the referees. Since it was legal, there wasn't much the refs could do except have the Hawks' trainer smooth the exposed edges with tape.

My knee felt strange when I got up from the banging. As a professional athlete I'd become accustomed to minor physical discomfort. That's all I thought this was. The knee didn't hurt. I could run on it, so I continued playing. I played the next night and again two nights later and felt fine. But on the fifth night, Tom LaGarde of the Dallas Mavericks, another seven-footer, collided into me and banged the same knee.

This time I heard a little clicking noise. With each step, the knee clicked. Damn, I thought, this is strange. But it still didn't hurt. I shrugged the incident off and finished the game. The knee stiffened up on me the next day—an off day—and was still stiff at shoot-around the following morning. I couldn't extend my left leg fully. And I continued to hear that strange click.

Whirlpool treatment didn't loosen the knee up, so Dr. Kerlan checked it out before a game against Kansas City. He suspected there was something wrong but could not positively identify it. He said I should play. If something was wrong, the damage was already done.

I found out for sure early in the second period. While trying to cut with my man, Hawkeye Whitney, every part of my body moved but the knee. It said, "Sorry, but I'm not going with you." I heard something snap. After I left the game, Kerlan made the preliminary diagnosis: torn cartilage. He said he'd recommend surgery if the tear was as extensive as he thought. He hoped the ligament wasn't damaged, which would be a more severe injury.

Dr. Kerlan and his staff conducted a complete examination the next morning. When he showed me X rays from the arthrogram, my heart—everything—dropped. All night I'd been hoping I'd just have a sprained knee as I did my rookie season. If Dr. Kerlan read my disappointment, he didn't react to it. He continued on, doctorlike. He recommended immediate surgery to remove the cartilage and arranged for Dr. Steve Lombardo to perform the operation. He said the recovery would take longer if I allowed the knee to heal by itself and that he could not guarantee the results. He couldn't guarantee the results of the operation, either, but said my chances of a faster and more complete recovery would be better if I had one. This was on a Wednesday; Dr. Kerlan wanted Dr. Lombardo to operate the following Monday.

"If we remove the cartilage right away, you should be fit for the playoffs," he said. "And don't worry. When you recover, you should be able to continue your career where you left off. Be thankful you didn't tear a ligament."

Despite the comforting words, I was miserable. I'd been playing so well. Through twenty games, we had a 15–5 record, and I was tenth in the league in scoring and first in both steals and assists.

I had arrived at training camp confident and strong, still glowing and drawing energy from our having won the league championship my rookie season. The summer didn't pass fast enough for me, and neither did training camp. I'd enjoyed winning the championship so much, I wanted to get back and do it again. I felt I had total command of my game and opened all the valves.

Kareem, after a lackluster preseason, started slowly. But the rest of us picked up the slack and handled it, allowing him a rare opportunity to sit back and enjoy the show. For once he didn't have to shoulder most of the pressure. I'm sure he appreciated the break.

Jimmy Chones was playing especially well. We called him "Crusher" because he crushed everybody under the boards.

Coming off a mediocre regular season and a poor playoffs, he came to camp lean and mean, intent on making a bigger contribution. He showed some of his toughness during a few head-to-head battles with Kareem in training-camp scrimmages. Kareem rarely is challenged in camp and wasn't ready for Jimmy's. He angrily threw the ball at Jimmy and stalked out of one practice, and Westhead had to stop another just as the battle was heating up. Coach should have let it go. Jim was playing hard, that's all, and giving Kareem a workout. Somebody had to. Everybody needs a challenge. Like when Coop guards me, that's a challenge.

My only down period—before the injury—came when Kareem rejoined the team after being poked in the eye, an injury that sidelined him two games. I worked overtime those nights he was hurt, playing forty-seven minutes one game and forty-one the next. It caught up with me a couple of days later. When he came back, I played terribly, and we lost to Portland, our first loss after opening the season with five straight wins. I was tired and miserable that night.

Then, a few weeks later, came the injury. My father and Tuck flew out to spend some time with me before the operation. We talked about it a lot, and also talked about the possibility of not going through with it because of the emotional strain of surgery and the subsequent rehabilitation. We got philosophical at times. We discussed the relationship between mind and body and how, if I had the operation, I'd be tested mentally as I'd never been before.

Because I'd grown so quickly as a kid, sore knees were a common problem for me. That's one reason I don't like to run just for the sake of running. I've never been the jogging type.

"You're going to have to run," Tuck said.

"I know," I said. "I'll run."

"You say that now. But I've seen how you run. Like an old man."

"I'm telling you. If I have to run, I'll run."

"I know. And I'm telling you this is going to be the toughest thing you've ever done in your life. You have to be totally dedicated. If you aren't, forget about making it back this season. You can't run halfway and say, 'That's enough for today.' You gotta go all out.

"And," Tuck continued, "if you aren't together upstairs . . ." He tapped his temple. "You may never make it back."

"I'll make it back," I snapped. "I'll make it back this season." I was depressed enough already; I didn't need a lecture. But Tuck, being the psychologist, was already turning my head away from the injury and towards the rehabilitation. "I'll even outrun you if I have to," I said. "I can do that any time."

"Okay," he said. "I'll put together a running program and work out with you. We'll see."

We decided to go ahead with the operation. As far as I was concerned, there wasn't any choice. I wanted to rejoin the team and play as soon as I could.

Those first two weeks were the worst. I wore a cast from my toes to my groin. All I did was lie around the apartment feeling sorry for myself and watching television. It didn't take me long to memorize the television schedule—I knew what program was on which station at what time during the week. I wanted to bang the walls. I got so mad a couple of times, I screamed. I'm not the type to lie around the house all day. I like to go out, be active, do things. Not being able to walk killed me. People see my smile and picture me being like that all the time. That's part of me but not all of me. I have my down moments, just like anybody else.

It's like part of me is Magic Johnson and another is Earvin Johnson. When I'm playing ball, I'm Magic in the people's eyes, but I'm Earvin to myself. Reporters see me as Magic and probably don't realize they're listening to Earvin. I'm Magic to the people in L.A. but Earvin to my friends in Lansing—except when we're playing cards and I'm winning every hand. That's the Magic of Earvin.

Being alone for so long, longer than I'd ever been before, gave me time to reflect. I thought about my life, about the good times—which far outnumbered the bad times—and tried to put it all into perspective. It was like taking a time-out. And it wasn't until I took the time-out that I realized how much I needed it. Things had happened so fast that I hadn't had the time to enjoy them. It was as though I had been wolfing down a fine meal instead of savoring it. Winning the NCAA championship hadn't sunk in, let alone winning the pro title. At twenty-one, it hadn't occurred to me that I had better make the time to enjoy the things coming my way. For the first time I felt vulnerable. It hit me: "Hey, it can go quickly." When my time comes, I want to have enjoyed life to its fullest; I want to have had as much fun as 20,000 people put together.

While I'm not a regular churchgoer anymore, I've always been spiritual. It may seem like a weak excuse, but in L.A. I haven't had the time to go because of basketball. Because we play almost every Sunday night, we have shoot-arounds Sunday mornings. That doesn't mean I believe in God any less. The main reason I don't go to church regularly is that I feel I can believe within myself. Having come from a family in which different kinds of faith were affirmed, I learned that belief in itself is far more important than how or where or when the belief is practiced.

I felt much better as soon as the cast came off. Finally, I could move around. I went straight to the Forum to watch a game that first night. Just the idea of being back with the guys lifted my spirits. Throughout the two weeks in the cast, I couldn't wait to hang out in the locker room and sit on the bench. Sitting there in street clothes didn't even bother me.

I picked a heck of a night for my first time. The Lakers had lost three straight games, and five of eight since I'd injured my knee. Westhead decided it was time to shake up the lineup.

As Westhead began issuing defensive assignments for that

night's game against the Utah Jazz, I sat on the stool in front of my locker. I felt great. Most of the guys did stretching exercises on the floor.

"Norman," said Westhead, "you're on Billy McKinney. Butch, you've got Griffith . . ."

Butch? Everybody looked around. Mouths dropped to the floor in astonishment. Butch was rookie guard Butch Carter, a second-round draft choice from Indiana. Butch would make his first NBA start as Coop's replacement.

"Kareem," said Westhead. He continued as though nothing had happened. "You guard Ben Poquette. Brew, you're on. . . ."

Brew? Again everything stopped. Guys looked around shaking their heads. But nobody said anything. Brew was Jim Brewer, a veteran power forward picked up the day before the start of the regular season. He was replacing Jim Chones. I'm wondering what's going on here. Westhead finished the defensive assignments, and that was it. No explanation.

I sat next to Michael on the bench, and I could tell he was fuming. He didn't say a word. He didn't have to—his anguish was written all over his face. After the game, both Jimmy and Coop went after Norm and wore his ear out. But Norm didn't know any more than they did. Nobody could believe the way it went down. It blew Jimmy away. He was having a great season—his best—and was the team's leading rebounder, just ahead of Kareem.

With Jimmy it was like: "What did I do? Is Brew going to get eleven rebounds because I'm only getting ten? Did I do something, or what?" He felt he, along with Coop, was being singled out for punishment and didn't know why.

Westhead never communicated with the guys. He should have given them the courtesy of an explanation. "Hey, Jim. I want to try this." That's all he had to say. You can't come out one day and—bam! bam!—just do it and expect everybody to accept it enthusiastically. Westhead might have made the right move, but he did it wrong.

Reporters pressed him for an explanation and he said: "Basically, what we're trying to do is create a better balance of energy."

Coop was quiet. He dressed quickly and left. Chones, on the other hand, lingered in the locker room and sounded off to the press.

"I don't know how to take it," he said. "It upset me the way it was done. Why me? I've been playing my ass off. I've been dominating just about every big man I've played at my position. I've been boarding. I've done everything I've ever been asked to do.

"It's ridiculous, man. I guess it's easier to set me down than somebody else. I'm just upset, very upset. I'm not going to hide my feelings. I'm playing the best I've ever played in my life, and there's no way I can accept this silently. I give everything in my heart to this team. I find it hard to believe this is the kind of respect I'm shown."

I had a feeling Jimmy was going to talk after the game. He had to get it off his chest. He knew he couldn't talk to the coach. As he said, he was a very upset basketball player. The entire time Chones talked, Westhead watched from across the room. I don't know what was going through his mind. I knew he didn't believe in Jimmy. They'd had their problems before, including that sidelines shouting match during a game against Milwaukee the previous season.

With the Balance of Energy lineup, as the press called it, we won five straight. As soon as we lost, Westhead put Chones back in the lineup. But Coop continued to come off the bench for another two weeks. During those last two weeks, we won only 3 of 9 games. From the time of my injury until early January, when Coop returned to the starting lineup, we had an 11–11 record. From then till February 27—the day I rejoined the team—we won 17 of 23 games.

My rehabilitation process began the day after the operation, starting with simple—yet difficult—exercises like putting small amounts of pressure on my toes. As that got easier, I moved on to tougher exercises. And on and on. As soon as the cast was removed, I began working out at Dr. Kerlan's institute twice daily, six times a week. It was excruciating and difficult work, but I just gritted my teeth and continued, trying to distract myself from the pain by dreaming of the final result—the moment I'd step back on court in a Laker uniform. I was totally committed to the rehabilitation. I knew I'd make it back if I worked hard. Even while visiting Lansing for eight days over Christmas and New Year's I continued the therapy prescribed by Dr. Kerlan and his staff.

Once the knee was strong enough, I returned to Lansing to begin the running program designed by Tuck. He joined me as promised. I surprised him. He'd never seen me run the way I did those cold Michigan mornings. He knew I was serious—I didn't slack off once. When it's for real, I suck it up and get the job done. No fooling around. I was on time every morning. Tuck wasn't.

"Hey," I said, "you're late. I've been waiting here ten minutes. Where've you been?"

Tuck had just driven up in his Jeep. He was putting on his running shoes.

"I'm already warmed up," I said.

"Okay," he said, quickly tying his shoes. "I'm ready. Let's go."

And we were off. Tuck worried I'd overdo it; that's how dedicated I was.

"Take it easy going around the curves," he warned me one morning.

"I've taken it easy long enough."

I was coming back, and the closer I got, the faster I wanted to go. By the first week in February I could sense the end was in sight. What an exhilarating feeling. I caught up with the team in Indianapolis and joined the workouts for two days. That was fun. Back with the boys on the road. While my wind needed work, as I knew it would, my quickness and maneuverability were better than I expected. I tried a few of my old moves and felt so relieved when they worked. I wasn't all the way back by any means, but I held my own.

A week later, Dr. Kerlan examined the knee and told me it was healed. At that point, the problem was my wind more than my knee. It was time to get into shape. Dr. Kerlan notified Dr. Buss of my passing marks and told him I could begin playing February 20—in ten days. But Buss, who'd been cautious all along, moved my return back one week. By then, another week didn't matter to me. It was just around the corner.

Pat Riley volunteered to put the finishing touches to my rehabilitation. He was going to see to it that I got into game shape.

"You're going to need this," Pat told me before we began our workouts. "There will come a time when you can't get tired. You may be playing your fortieth minute and you may be beat, but we won't be able to give you a breather because the game will be on the line. In order for you to be ready then, you must pay the price now."

I nodded. I knew what he was talking about. I also knew how it felt. I'd never let my team down in the past and wouldn't in the future.

"It's up to you," he continued. "You have to work on your own to get into shape. But I'll help. I'll work you as hard as I can and as hard as you want me to."

"That's what I want, Riles," I said.

Wind sprints. Defensive sliding drills. Rebounding. Thirty to forty-five minutes every day after the team's regular practice. Riley put me through one drill where I had to dunk from one side, come down with the ball, dunk on the other side, come down with the ball, and continue dunking until I couldn't dunk anymore. In the beginning I could do only six or seven dunks. By the time I was set to rejoin the team, I was doing twenty at a crack. It took a lot of time, sweat, and work to do it. I don't know how many times I wanted to throw the ball at Riley and scream, "That's enough!" But I never did.

"You okay?" Riley asked me once.

I had just finished the dunking drill and he wanted me to go again. I was exhausted. I paused to catch a couple of seconds' rest and he was asking me if I was okay. I wanted to strangle him. I took a deep breath and glared.

"Yeah, I'm okay," I said. "What do you want?"

"What do you want?" was his rejoinder. We'd been going through this routine. "You want to go another dunk?"

"What do you want?" I wasn't going to tell him I'd had enough. I'd go until I collapsed, if that's what he wanted. But I wasn't going to volunteer.

"One more time," he said, "then that'll be it for the day. Okay?"

Despite the team's success in January and February, much of the harmony that existed during the championship season had eroded before I rejoined the team. Some hostility continued to linger from Westhead's Balance of Energy lineup. Chones was never the same again. In Westhead's system, the power forward was strictly a rebounder. His role in the offense was minimal; all he did was pass and set picks.

Chones, who could shoot the medium-range jumper, rarely had an opportunity to do so, since he was the last option in the offense. Had he been encouraged to shoot the jumper, he could have added another dimension to the offense and taken some of the heat off the pivot. But even though he didn't like the way he was being used, Chones didn't complain publicly again. He had said it all in December. He just worked his shift and went home. He acted like a man whose will was broken.

I came back to face the problems the team was having— and my return helped create new problems. We never really jelled. And the season ended with that nightmare— our elimination by Houston from the playoffs when I missed the shot near the end that could have won the game and the series for us.

After my knee surgery, doctors and physical therapists

had told me not to worry about the mental adjustment. That was impossible. Many times during my rehabilitation, I'd stay awake nights, wondering if I'd make it back. The next morning I'd mention it to Dr. Kerlan or to the physical therapist and be reassured that everything would be all right. But even when the injury heals, you don't know for sure. It's natural to hold back. The strength of the knee is meaningless if the mind remains unconvinced.

And no matter how hard you try to convince yourself that the knee is fine and you're not afraid, you may still hold something back. That something—perhaps a split second of hesitation—can prevent complete recovery. Some athletes never make the mental adjustment. Those who don't eventually fade away. It's scary.

About three weeks after the season ended I finally signed the extension to my contract. It had been sitting around for more than two months. But I couldn't sign it in good conscience until I knew for sure my knee was all right.

Dr. Buss had first talked to me about the extension the previous summer. He had already extended the contracts of Jamaal, Norm, and Coop and wanted to put mine into the same time frame as theirs. He was talking about a one- or two-year extension.

"Fine," I told him. "Sounds great."

He smiled. He hadn't come down from the high of winning the 1980 NBA championship the month before. Neither had I. "We'll do it," he said. "Let's get together later in the summer and work out the details."

My original plan was to finish my career in the Midwest, in either Detroit or Chicago. But after my rookie season I had a new plan. I liked Los Angeles, the franchise, the Forum, the players, and the owner. What more could I ask for? I wanted to be a Laker for life, which I discussed with my family, Tuck, and George and Harold Andrews. I also wanted to avoid free agentry. Representatives of several teams had already made sly overtures to me, saying, essentially, that they had loads of money to offer me when my contract ran its course. I just wanted to play ball; I didn't want to go through the meat market. I had had enough of that in choosing a college.

Buss was receptive to the idea of a lifetime contract. "Obviously I hadn't considered this," he told George and Harold later that summer, "but I'd be very happy to. Let me work up some numbers and get back to you."

There was no rush. Buss was in the middle of several other business transactions, one being the purchase of the Pickfair estate in Beverly Hills. I didn't hear from him until training camp. There, he outlined the $25-million, 25-year contract.

I just laughed when he told me about it. We were sitting in his apartment at the Ocotillo Lodge in Palm Springs. He laughed, too.

"Sounds great to me," I said.

"I'll set up a meeting with George and Harold and get the ball rolling," he said.

That meeting was scheduled to take place in Phoenix on Monday, November 24, 1980, which, ironically, turned out to be the same day I had knee surgery. The previous Satur day, Harold met Buss at a Lakers-Suns game in Phoenix.

"Is Monday's meeting still on?" Harold asked.

"Yes," Buss said, "it definitely is."

Dr. Buss easily could have delayed the negotiations for months, perhaps a year, to see how I responded to surgery. I certainly would have understood. But he never hedged. He met with George and Harold as scheduled and established the parameters of the contract. Over the next few months, Harold and Jerry Fine, Dr. Buss's attorney, as principal combatants, and George, as referee, hammered out the details of the richest and longest-running contract in sports history.

I knew I'd have to live up to it. I didn't know I'd have to live with it hanging over my head.

13

Back on Top

CHAMPIONSHIP SERIES—1981–82

June 9, 1982

I woke up this morning with a smile. I continued grinning as I sat up in bed. I couldn't help it. It wouldn't turn off. We did it, I thought. We really did it. Wow, what a feeling.

I began thinking back to the troubles when Westhead was fired early in the season. To the start of the playoffs— the Phoenix series, which we won in four straight. Then to the San Antonio series. We were awesome in that one, too. As soon as the Spurs made two or three mistakes, we pounced on them and made them pay. Two hoops, three hoops, four hoops in a row. First one guy, then another guy. We always had somebody else doing the job. Against San Antonio, we geared our defense to contain two players, George Gervin and Mike Mitchell. But the Spurs couldn't concentrate on only two Laker players. We had too many guns. Maybe they could slack off Rambis, who was primarily a banger, but who else? Norm? Mac? Kareem? Silk? Coop? Me? Not a chance.

Before leaving Los Angeles, where we played and won the first two games, San Antonio coach Stan Albeck had said, "Wait until we get 'em before our 16,000 crazed fans at HemisFair Arena." I guess he thought a change of scenery would make a difference. It was wishful thinking. The fans, though a little crazed (particularly the rowdy "Baseline Bums"), didn't bother us. They're good fans—loyal, enthusiastic, and knowledgeable. They appreciate good basketball. We won two straight in San Antonio, giving us another sweep. No NBA team had ever before swept consecutive best-of-seven series.

George Gervin couldn't believe us. "Slow down," he said to me during one game. He knew we were good and probably would win the series, but he never thought we'd sweep. Once he realized we might sweep, he did everything within his power to prevent it. And he put on an incredible show for the San Antonio fans, scoring a total of 77 points those last two games.

"The Lakers are at a level that is just unbelievable," Albeck said. "Through all my years in professional basketball, I can't remember a team that played as well and as hard as they. I like their chances of winning it all. Sweeping Phoenix, then us, is not easy. Hell, they may be the best the league has ever seen. They have seven great athletes who never stop applying the pressure. They're not satisfied with the jump shot off the fast break. They keep pushing until they get the lay-up."

But even though we'd just eliminated his team and he'd said how great we were, Albeck still wasn't completely sold. "Because they're playing such perfect basketball," he said, "I wonder how they'll react to a loss. They have a lot of fragile personalities on that team. Will they come apart? That's a legitimate question."

As a Laker assistant coach under Jerry West for three years, Albeck was well acquainted with Kareem, Norman, and Silk. But I don't believe their relationships with him had any bearing on his skepticism. His feelings reflected those of many people around the league. Few believed in us because of our collapse against Houston the year before. But the idea of beating ourselves this time was out of the question. We had put Houston and last season behind us, though others hadn't. Our sights were riveted to what was straight ahead. This Laker team was in a far different frame of mind.

"Magic is changing his game around," Norm told reporters after we eliminated the Spurs. "He's sacrificing his offense by going to the boards more and getting the ball out."

I appreciated Norm saying that. He'd had a great series, averaging twenty-six points and killing San Antonio point-guard Johnny Moore in the process. His praise of my game exemplified that different frame of mind and how deeply committed we were to one another. Everybody did what had to be done for the Lakers to win. That's why my game changed during the playoffs. It wasn't a planned adjustment. With Mac coming off the bench and playing consistently well, we had plenty of shooters. So I became more conscious of keeping the ball moving and crashing the boards, particularly the offensive boards. I rarely looked for the shot unless I was down low. But it depended on the circumstances of the game. When I had to score, I did. Basically, I just tried to fill in the blanks.

We were confident we'd beat either Boston or Philadelphia, the Eastern Conference finalists. As Coop so eloquently phrased it, "The way we're playing right now, we can beat anybody. Bring on the Harlem Globetrotters."

Bring on somebody. Anybody.

We finished San Antonio on Saturday night. The next afternoon, Philadelphia beat Boston to take a 3–1 series lead in the East. Initially, I preferred playing the Celtics in the league finals since they were defending champs. Once they fell so far behind, I switched my allegiance to the 76ers. I wanted their series to end as quickly as possible so ours could begin. I was hyped and ready to go. Waiting frustrated and unnerved me, and I started worrying that we'd lose our momentum even though we had already handled layoffs of nine and seven days. We had good workouts early in the week—long, hard, and intense—as Riley began preparing us for Philadelphia. Everybody was emotionally charged.

Philadelphia and Boston played again Wednesday. I was pulling for the 76ers to wrap it up that night. If not that night, I was hoping they'd win Friday. Either way, we'd begin the finals Sunday. The last thing I wanted to see was a suspenseful series. If Boston won, then won again Friday, the finals wouldn't begin until the following Thursday, which would mean a twelve-day layoff for us. I didn't think I could last that long. I was antsy.

I was also frustrated by a couple of nagging injuries. One, an old ankle sprain that I'd twisted during Wednesday's practice. And two, the jammed middle three knuckles on my right hand, my shooting hand. I first jammed them going for a steal during the third game of the Phoenix series. Dennis Johnson, trying to protect the ball, instinctively slammed my hand with his elbow. From then on, I banged them at least once a game. Ice packs would usually relieve the pain and allow me to continue playing.

When you play as hard as you can—which is the only way I know—and you're constantly digging out loose balls and battling on the boards, you find that injuries are inevitable. Still, they depress you because they inhibit the way you play your game.

The injuries were a nuisance, but the wait was intolerable. I didn't know what to do with myself. All I could think about was getting on with the finals. Boston won on

Wednesday, and by the end of the week everybody was restless. Friday, the day of the sixth game, Riley assembled us after practice.

"If Philly wins tonight," he said, "we fly out first thing tomorrow morning. If Philly loses . . ."

I groaned. Everybody laughed.

"I know how you feel, Magic," Riley said. "If Philly loses, I don't want to see you guys until Monday. Go someplace and try to forget about basketball."

I made plane reservations to leave for Lansing that night. If we were going to have to wait any longer, I figured I'd better get out of town before I lost all my friends. I was so uptight. As soon as somebody mentioned anything about basketball, I'd just turn off. It was the last thing I wanted to talk about. I wasn't very good company, and that wasn't me. My friends didn't deserve that kind of treatment.

Sure enough, Boston beat the 76ers in Philadelphia to force a seventh game Sunday. That was it. I flew home and moved in with my parents for the weekend. It was the best thing I could have done. Instead of calling on friends all over town, as I usually did, I stayed home and relaxed. My mom and dad, having seen me like this before, took care of me and untied the emotional knots. I was thankful I had them to turn to. Mom cooked some delicious dishes for me and topped them off with her great sweet-potato pie. She made me eat everything. Then she tried giving me seconds.

"No more," I said as she put another plate in front of me that Saturday night. "I can't eat any more."

"Eat up, Junior," she said.

"No, Mom. I'm full."

"Look how skinny you are. Doesn't anybody feed you out there?"

I was skinny. At 204, I weighed ten pounds less than I had at the start of the season. But I liked playing light. It made me quicker and more mobile. Because of that, I became a better rebounder.

I couldn't sit still while watching the seventh game on television Sunday afternoon. After about two minutes, I left home and made the ten-minute drive to Tuck's house. I walked through the front door and went downstairs to the television room. My father and Tuck were watching the game on a huge screen.

"What's the score?" I asked.

"Seventeen-eight," my father said.

"Who's winning?"

"Philadelphia."

We watched in silence for a few moments.

On the screen, Dr. J. tapped the ball away from Larry Bird and scored a lay-in at the other end of the court on a pass from Andrew Toney.

"Do it, Doc," said Tuck. "Make that housecall."

"I think Philly's going to do it," my father said.

"Mmmmm," said Tuck. "You might be right."

I entered the adjacent room and looked around. It was incredible. It was not your normal recreation room. Tuck had converted it into a small basketball court. It had hardwood floors and a regulation basket hung at the proper height. It also had vaulted ceilings roomy enough for some serious shooting. Tuck sometimes would shoot by himself into the early-morning hours.

I reentered the television room and started walking out.

"Where are you going?" Tuck asked.

"Home," I said.

At home, I watched awhile, then drove back to Tuck's.

"What's the score?" I asked as I entered. On the screen, Bird made a fifteen-foot jumper.

"If he gets it going," Tuck said, turning to my father, "watch out."

My father grunted.

"What's that make it?" I asked again.

"Thirty-four–thirty-two, Sixers," said Tuck.

"How much time?"

"Halfway through the second period."

I nodded and watched. After a few minutes, I turned and started to leave.

"Hey," my father said, "you going home again?"

"Yeah," I said. From upstairs I could hear Tuck say, "I think he's ready to go, Mr. Johnson."

I was, too. I had a reservation to fly to L.A. early Monday morning, but changed it as soon as Philadelphia won. I flew back that night, feeling much better knowing who our opponent would be and after a weekend at home with my folks.

Spirits were high when the team returned to work the next morning. Practice Monday, practice Tuesday, fly to Philadelphia Wednesday and play Thursday. The finals were right around the corner. The only distraction that first day was the uproar over Boston coach Bill Fitch's comment. "It's too bad," he was quoted as saying, "because we would have beaten the Lakers."

All the L.A. writers elicited our reactions. I was mad. I couldn't believe he'd put us down like that. We'd never done anything to him. Essentially, he was saying that if we beat Philadelphia, it wouldn't prove anything. We had to beat the Celtics to be recognized as real champs. It made all of us mad. He could have had some dignity in defeat.

"I don't know what to say," I told reporters. "I'd like to know how he plans to prove it."

The layoff had taken its toll, as I was afraid it would. We got off to a bad start against Philadelphia in Game 1. I got winded quickly and actually gasped for breath on several occasions. From a conditioning standpoint, there's a considerable difference between practicing and playing a game. You notice it immediately. Our sharpness and timing were gone. The 76ers led by 11 at halftime and expanded the lead to 15 midway through the third period.

Then suddenly it all came back. Silk started it with a lay-in and two free throws. Kareem followed with a skyhook, Nixon with a free throw, Nixon again with a jumper off the fast break, and then Kareem with another skyhook. Eleven straight points! In only two and a half minutes we got back into the game. That's moving. After Caldwell Jones scored for the 76ers, we ran off eight more quick points.

"Let's keep it rolling," Norm said as he came to the bench for a time-out. "We got 'em now. You can see it in their eyes."

We stunned them. It happened so fast, they didn't know what hit them. It was our one-two punch—the half-court trap and fast break. In four minutes, we outscored them 19–2 to take the lead; after ten minutes, it was 40–9. Then we eased up and coasted home with the victory, our ninth straight in the playoffs. By doing so, we tied a league record for the most consecutive playoff wins and set the record for most in a single season. The reporters started talking about the possibility of a complete sweep. We talked about it, too. We wanted it. So did Riley. "Go for it," he told us.

"I think everybody recognizes that this is a chance of a lifetime, a chance to go down in history," Silk said. "If we do it, we have to be considered one of the best teams ever. Whether we can or not is another matter. Personally, I think we can."

I had my doubts. Except for the ten-minute burst, we hadn't even approached the level of excellence we'd achieved against Phoenix and San Antonio. Game 2 would be the key, I thought. If we played well and got through that one, we'd do it.

But we didn't. The 76ers wouldn't let us. They played great defense, holding us to under 100 points for the first time in the playoffs, and handed us our first defeat in forty-eight days—since April 13, when Golden State beat us. Forget the sweep.

Julius Erving, who played well the first game, rose to the occasion and played even better the second. Every time we'd threaten to make a move and seize the momentum, he'd respond with a big play to slow us down. Normally an average rebounder, he killed us on the boards, especially on the offensive end. The offensive rebound frustrates the defense. You work your tail off to force the offense into taking a poor percentage shot. If it misses and you lose the rebound, all your work is wasted. Nobody was boxing Dr. J off the offensive boards. Pat Riley decided that would be my job as the series shifted to Los Angeles for Games 3 and 4.

So far, we had been successful in containing Andrew Toney, the 76ers' high-scoring guard. Although not as consistent a scorer as the Doc, he can be more explosive. We had witnessed one of his major eruptions back in March. That day, coming off the bench as third guard behind Maurice Cheeks and Lionel Hollins, Toney ripped off 20 points in the fourth quarter alone, and scored 46 for the game to lead Philadelphia to a come-from-behind win. He burned everybody who tried to stop him, baffling even Coop, our defensive stopper.

"We tried everything but saw off his arms and poke out his eyes," Michael said after that game. "What can you do? He can be a bitch. Once he got it rolling, all Philly did was clear out for him. You have to give him something sometimes. You play him for the jumper or the drive. You can't play him for both, because he's too good."

Toney, who had moved into the starting lineup when Hollins injured a hand earlier in the playoffs, had a couple of explosions in the Boston series, including a 34-pointer in the seventh game. By the time that series was through, reporters were calling him "the Boston Strangler." Toney didn't scare us, though. After going against George Gervin, the Iceman—the best—we weren't afraid of anybody.

While I started each of the first two games guarding Toney, Norm, Coop, and Silk each took his turn. Toney scored 20 the first game and 12 the second. But we didn't count him out. We knew he'd make his presence felt before the series was over.

Another player in the spotlight was Kurt Rambis. Members of the media from all over the country cover the NBA finals, and many of them were discovering Kurt for the first time. Which was good. He deserved the recognition. For a halftime feature CBS asked him to come out of a telephone booth wearing a cape to jazz up the interview. Because of his thick-framed glasses, we called him Clark Kent. CBS thought it would be a good idea to cash in on the Superman theme.

Kurt thought it was a little too weird and turned it down. "I make a fool of myself without even trying," he said jokingly. "I don't see why I should consciously contribute to it."

Back home we played our best basketball of the series. We tore into the 76ers with the trap and fast break and opened a 20-point lead two minutes into the second period of Game 3. The easy win made everybody feel better. If Stan Albeck or anybody else had still been wondering how we'd react to a loss, we'd satisfied his curiosity.

Norm bounced back with a big offensive game after making only three of fourteen shots in Game 2. Norm was upset in Game 2 because Maurice Cheeks kept bumping his elbow to throw off his jump shot. Complaining to the refs didn't help, so he took his case to Cheeks right after the game. I could see him pointing and shaking his finger at Cheeks.

"What did you say?" I asked.

"I told him he'd better not do it again," Norm said.

Cheeks must have taken heed of the warning because Norman didn't complain in Game 3. He went for 29.

As instructed, I concentrated on boxing Dr. J. off the boards, a job I succeeded in doing. The Doc, who had 23 rebounds the first two games, grabbed only three in this one. I felt I had contributed to minimizing his effectiveness and was proud of it. It was one of those accomplishments that usually go unnoticed.

But not by everybody. Riley, for one, had noticed.

"Magic has taken it upon himself to give the team what it needs," he said. "His impact on a game is incredible. Because of his great intelligence, court sense, and instinct, he never comes downcourt with a preconceived idea of what to do. Like, he doesn't come down figuring, 'Okay, I'm going to shoot this one,' and block out all other options. He looks around, sizes up the situation, and makes the play. Almost always he makes the right one.

"If he were selfish, he would score thirty every night. But he knows that is unnecessary. He only takes what is there. Only when the game hangs in balance does he intently look for the shot, and that's when I want him to look for it. He's the most disciplined offensive player I've ever seen."

I was touched. Above everything else, I've always tried to be a team player. Riley was telling me I was doing the job.

We got off to another fast start in Game 4. But this time the 76ers didn't go without a struggle. They came out with their own half-court trap the second half and worked it successfully. For a while, it looked like a rerun of Game 1 except for the shoe being on the other foot. They ran and forced the turnovers, not us. We were the ones who helplessly watched a big lead slip away. But unlike Philadelphia in Game 1, we didn't watch it *all* slip away. After the 76ers blew two chances to cut our lead to 5 points late in the game, we stiffened and pulled ahead to win by 10.

That was the big one. We were confident going back to Philly for Game 5 with a 3-1 lead. No team in league history had ever climbed out of that deep a hole to win a league championship series. We were back in the groove. Or, so we thought. The fifth game turned into a nightmare. A few questionable calls by the referees held us back in the beginning, preventing us from taking another quick start. Had we jumped out quickly, we might have snapped the 76ers' resolve.

Then, late in the first quarter, I got rapped across my sore knuckles while trying to make a steal from Toney. It was a bad one. Jack Curran treated my knuckles with ice as soon as I came out of the game, but the ice didn't ease the pain as it usually did. I played, but my hand hurt all night.

We simply collapsed the second half. Philadelphia outscored us 61–30 during the last eighteen minutes to win by 33. It was embarrassing. But it didn't shake our confidence. Instead, it fired us up. We talked about it on the flight home, and the more we talked about it, the more determined we became. We decided Game 6, Tuesday night in L.A., would be the winner.

It had been a long, painful season. Before it began, I had been confident that I'd fully recovered from the knee injury and would make people forget about the mini-series loss to Houston. But the hostility that came down on me after Paul Westhead was fired threw me. For the first time in my life I was hurt, as a fighter is hurt the first time he is knocked to the canvas. I got up wobbly and shaken. And I exhausted all my physical and emotional resources just trying to stay on my feet.

People had been telling me all season that winning the championship would be my vindication. But I wasn't seeking vindication. I wanted to win Game 6 for a deeper, more instinctive reason. It had nothing to do with Paul Westhead or the boos or the things written about me. I wanted to win for my teammates, for Dr. Buss and the Laker organization, for my family and friends, and for Laker fans everywhere. But I also wanted to win for a more personal reason—for the pure pleasure of it.

Winning was all I thought about Monday night. The championship was so close I could almost reach out and grab it. I got myself so psyched up I couldn't sleep and had to talk myself down. "Be patient. Take it easy. The game will be here before you know it. Relax. You'll do it. Easy, now. Get some sleep. . . ."

Usually I'm one of the last to arrive in the locker room

before a game. We're supposed to be there no later than an hour and a half before tip-off. On a normal night I'll walk through the door with a minute or two to spare. For Game 6, I was the first one there. All I could think about all day long was getting to the Forum and playing the game. When I ran out of things to do, I couldn't wait any longer.

The sparks flew in that locker room before the game. Guys came in smacking palms. "Okay, let's go. This is the night." Nobody mentioned the possibility of a seventh game. If this had been Game 37 of the regular season, players would have been into their own things. Some would have been talking, others reading the pregame stats. A few would have been quiet, bothered perhaps by problems going down on the home front or preoccupied by thoughts totally unrelated to basketball. The atmosphere for a big game is different; at least it was for this one. It was all business. As game time approached, the guys grew quiet. The only sounds were the strains of soft jazz and R & B from several tape cassettes. Each player concentrated in his own way. You could feel the tension.

I lay flat on my back, staring at the ceiling. I flexed my right hand. The knuckles seemed fine. They'd have to be. It was winning time. Besides, the whole hand was numb from the day's ice treatments. Other players stretched. Kareem, who'd been having recurring migraine headaches and had missed shoot-around that morning, sat on his stool, thinking and gazing straight ahead. He looked so serious that Riley thought he had another headache and sent Curran over to check him out. Kareem shook his head. He was all right.

"You've done everything you've had to do to get to this day," Riley said in his pregame talk. "You turned back Seattle. You eliminated Phoenix and San Antonio. You split in Philadelphia, then held service at home. You went back and tried to win Game 5 and didn't. So this is it. The buck stops right here. . . ."

Riley looked around the room before continuing. A cigarette dangled from his hand. The room was still, all eyes on Riley.

"It stops with you," he said. "If you're going to win the championship, you're going to do it tonight in front of your fans and families. Let's go out there and take care of business."

We were pumped up. In less than two minutes, we scored four lay-ups and a free throw before Philadelphia could get on the scoreboard. Our fast start, so devastating to the 76ers in Games 3 and 4, didn't faze them this time. They thought they had broken us with the 33-point win and would beat us at the Forum.

Their confidence and our determination were the combustible elements that sparked the best and most emotional game of the series. Dr. J, who was having a great championship, personally put Philadelphia back into the game early in the third period by scoring his team's first eight points of the quarter. The last two hoops—a flying hesitation drive and a soaring left-handed tip-in off his own missed shot— were messages. First, he was telling his teammates that it was time to get moving; second, he was telling us to watch out.

If Philadelphia was the people's choice, it was because of Doc, one of the most popular and respected athletes in the country. He had missed in two previous trips to the finals— losing to Portland in 1977 and to us in 1980—and people wanted to see him win a championship ring. If he had been playing somebody else, I would have been rooting for him, too. He's one of the nicest guys you'd ever want to meet. He's a generous and caring man who isn't hung up on himself.

Despite Doc's firm prodding, the 76ers couldn't knock us out of the lead. The closest they came was seven minutes into the third period when Doc got the ball down low and took it up for the finger roll. Had he scored, Philly would have taken the lead. On the Laker bench, Riley stood and watched with apprehension, his hands poised to form the "T" to signal a time-out. Up to then he had declined to take one, thinking it would be a sign of weakness. Had Doc gotten the hoop, he would have had to. But just as Julius released the shot from point-blank range, Bob McAdoo soared in from behind and blocked it. It was the biggest play of the night. Philly never caught up, and we won, 114–104, our second championship in three years.

We went nuts in the locker room. For a few minutes after the game, we had it to ourselves, just the players, the coaches, and the trainer. We met in the middle of the room as we did after every game, win or lose, and huddled up. We put our hands in the center and walked our fingers all the way up, as high as we could reach, all the while going "Ooooooooooooooh. Oh!" Then we'd smack hands and do it again. It was sweet. We hugged and laughed. When the champagne was brought out, that was it. Champagne showers for everybody.

"Doo!" shouted Norm above the celebration. "Doo!" McAdoo, smiling, his face glistening from one part sweat, one part champagne, and one part victory, turned around. "Doo," Norm said again, "I told you you'd be in diamonds if you stuck with me."

Bob laughed. They met in the middle of the room and clasped hands. "You were right, Little Norm," he said.

Riley came over and embraced me. "Thanks, Magic," he said.

I smiled. I was happy. "It's my pleasure, Riles," I said, and we both laughed.

The moment and the immediate afterglow of victory are the most beautiful times I can imagine. For a brief spell, everything is in perfect order.

Real madness set in when the locker room doors were opened to the media. The crush was unbelievable. *Sport* magazine selected me as the series' Most Valuable Player. I was honored, and conveyed that to representatives of the magazine.

It is impossible for me to rate the championships I have won over the years. In its own way, each is special; this one because it represented, more so than the others, the strength, determination, and hard work of a group of guys who realized they would have to sacrifice individual glory for the good of the team in order to achieve their ends. The Lakers wanted the championship badly enough to make the required sacrifices. We paid the price—gladly. We knew it would be worth it to get back on top.

It's a nice place to be and, because of the nature of the difficulties that had to be overcome along the way, I appreciate being there more than ever before. It is never easy. There is no set route. But once you're there, it is always sweet.

Winning. To me, that's the magic.